Big Chinese Workbook for Little Hands

小手写中文

Written by Yang Yang

Consulting editors: Qin Chen, Claire Wang, Ke Peng, Yi Chen, Lai Yao

这是＿＿＿＿＿＿的书。

This book belongs to:

＿＿＿＿＿＿＿＿＿＿＿＿＿＿

ISBN: 978-1530080687

写给家长的话

为什么要先学笔画，再写字？

汉字里有六种基本笔画（点、横、竖、撇、捺、提）以及由它们组成和变体的几十种复合笔画。笔画是构成汉字的最小单位，每一种笔画都有自己的名称和书写顺序。孩子有了笔画的概念，才能真正学会写字，而不是"画"字。

黑体还是楷体？

楷体字最漂亮，几乎所有的传统教材都用楷体来教写字。可是当你放大一个楷体字，比如下面的"中文"，你会发现，它的每一笔都有藏头和回峰，并且粗细不均，是毛笔字的样子。对于四五岁初学写字的孩子来说，横平竖直是最大的要求。因此，我们在教学中选用黑体字打基础，而在配套的习字本中提供楷体字的对照练习，这样先学黑体后学楷体，当更加适应孩子的成长。

楷体 中文　中文 黑体

孩子需要先学会拼音才能使用这本书吗？

不需要。事实上我们更推崇汉字启蒙，但在这本练习册里提供生字注音，有两个用途：一是给家里不说中文的孩子做参考；二是给家里说中文的，并且已经认识一些汉字的孩子，帮助他们通过汉字来认识拼音。比如孩子已经认识"天"和"田"，现在看到它们的拼音是 tiān 和 tián，就会在脑子里产生印象，以后看到不认识的字"甜"tián 就可能念得出来。当然，这只是潜移默化的影响，本册练习对拼音部分不作要求。

几岁学写字比较好？每天写多少？

一般来说，五到六岁是开始学写汉字的理想年龄。将本书与《小手写中文 习字本》配套使用，每次可以做两页到四页的练习。

养成这样的习惯，学习效果会更好：

1. 每次做练习之前，都大声朗读上一次做过的部分，再默写一次写过的字。
2. 学写一个生字的时候，（在老师或家长的指导下）边写边说出笔画的名称。
比如写"口"的时候，就边写边说竖、横折、横。
3. 每个生字描写两遍、抄写一遍以后，就遮住写过的字，试着自己默写（最后两格）。
4. 鼓励孩子用每个生字组词或造句。

愿您的孩子从此学会写字、爱上中文！

Dear Parents,

The Chinese workbook that you have chosen, for your child, has been specifically designed for kids primarily living in English speaking countries and/or regions. So, congratulations to you, on finding a fun and intuitive workbook! Upon completion of this workbook, your child should be able to:

- Identify and write the 6 basic strokes and 19 most commonly used compound strokes in Chinese.
- Understand and adapt to the correct stroke order when writing Chinese characters.
- Distinguish colors and shapes in Chinese.
- Count from 1-1000.
- Talk briefly about dates relating towards age and the calendar.
- Understand, use and write the 8 most commonly used measure words in Chinese.
- Read up to 320 characters, and write 70+ of them, including 10 sight words that are most commonly used in Chinese.

Recommended usage: 2-4 pages at a time, two times a week. Read, review, and rewrite by memory the old characters before moving on to new exercises. A sound recording is available for most pages in this book. Scan the QR code on each page to listen to it. For more writing practice, please use *Tracing & Writing Chinese Characters, Level K,* which covers all characters in this book.

About the Author:

Ms. Yang Yang has been a children's language teacher for over 15 years. Her students won numerous awards in national English competitions in China. In 2006, she received her MA degree in Applied Linguistics from Ohio University with an Outstanding Teaching Award and an Outstanding Research Award in Second Language Acquisition. Then she did two years' PhD study in Chinese Linguistics at University of Arizona. She has been teaching Chinese at different universities and local Chinese schools since then and loved by her students. Currently she is also an invited writer and editor for *Little Pipa* (an educational magazine for young Chinese learners in the US).

About the Editors:

Ke Peng: President of Kentucky Association of Chinese Language Teachers, Associate Professor of Chinese, Department of Modern Languages, Western Kentucky University
Qin Chen: PhD of Modern Chinese Literature, Ohio State University
Claire Wang: Head of Foreign Language Programs, Accelerated Learning Laboratory, Arizona
Yi Chen: Teacher of Chinese Language and Culture, Confucius Institute, University of Arizona
Lai Yao: Teacher of Chinese Immersion program, Gavilan Peak School, Anthem, Arizona

Contents

笔画练习
Pre-writing Skills

héng

横 一

yī

èr

sān

Find and trace 横 ━ in these characters.

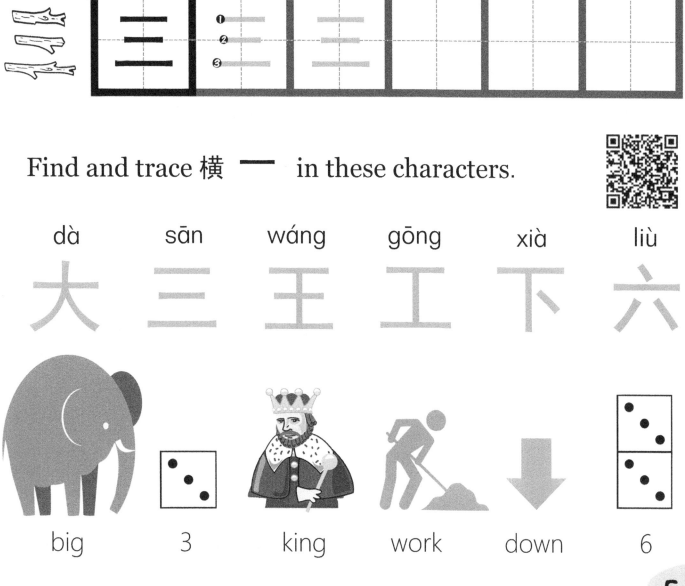

dà	sān	wáng	gōng	xià	liù
大	三	王	工	下	六
big	3	king	work	down	6

━ can be shorter or longer. Color the longer ━ lán sè 蓝色 blue color

and the shorter ━ hóng 红色 in each character.
red

shàng	tǔ	kāi	niú
上	土	开	牛
up	soil	open	cattle

Trace all the ━ you can find in each character. Then write down the number.

大 **1**　三 ☐　工 ☐　土 ☐

羊 ☐　天 ☐　走 ☐

yáng　tiān　zǒu

sheep, goat　sky, day　walk

6

shù
竖 丨

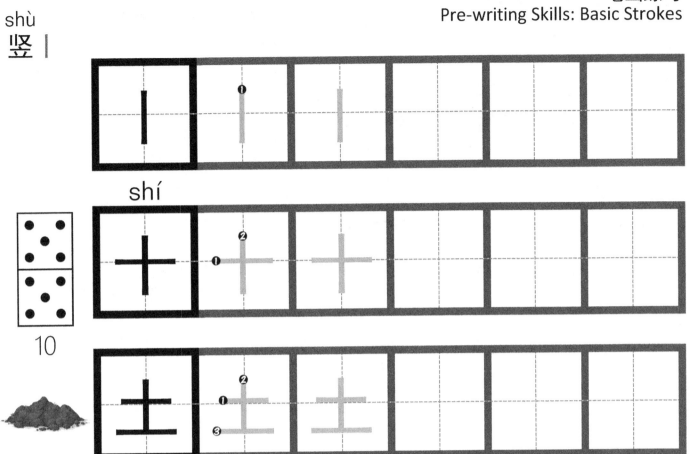

shí
十

10

土

Find and trace 竖 丨 in these characters.

mù

上 下 木 牛 羊 开

wood

Look at the characters, and circle those that have │.

天　下　三

rén　chē
牛　人　车
　people　vehicle

木　六　走

一 and │ make a 十. Can you find 十 in these characters? Trace them in this order ⚬┼.

hé　　tián　　mǐ　　　　shé

木　禾　田　米　王　舌

grain　field　rice　　tongue

piě

撇 can be standing ノ , sitting ノ , or lying down 一 .

chǎng

factory

qiān

1000

thousand

Find and trace 撇 ノ ノ 一 in these characters.

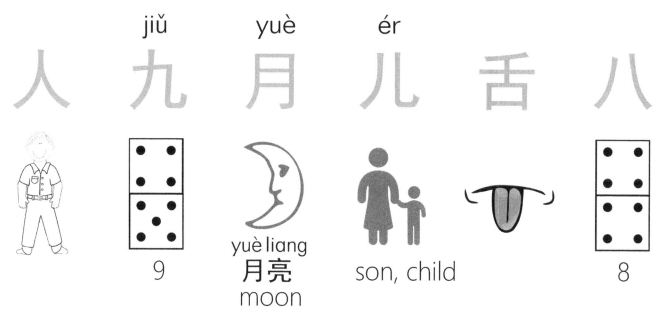

人　九
　　jiǔ
月
yuè
儿
ér
舌　八

9

yuè liang
月亮
moon

son, child

8

zhàn zhe　　zuò　　　　tǎng
站 着 ノ ， 坐 着 ノ ， 还 是 躺 着 一 ？
Standing,　　sitting,　　　or　lying down?

Help each character find its container. Draw a line.

nà
捺 乀

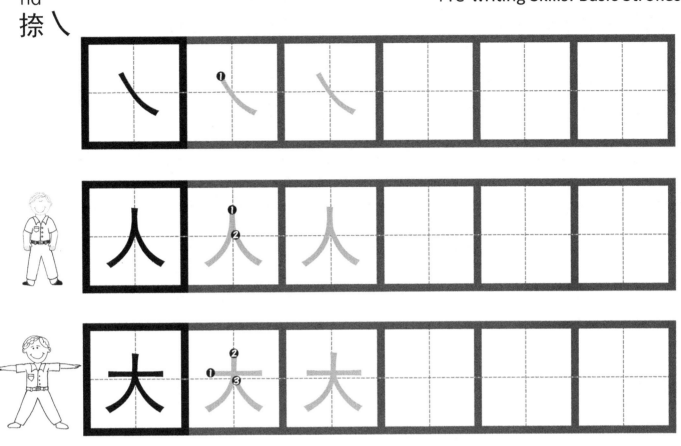

Find and trace 捺 乀 in these characters.

huǒ   cháng   guā

木　火　长　瓜　八　天

    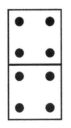

fire   long   melon

When a ╲ comes at the bottom of a character, it lies down like this ﹏. Can you find and trace the lying ﹏ ?

zú

guò

走

足

过

feet

pass

Stroke additions. Can you write down a character that is made of these strokes?

1. 一 + 丨 = ☐

2. 丿 + ╲ = ☐

3. 十 + 一 = ☐

4. 一 + 人 = ☐

5. 三 + 丨 = ☐

6. 二 + 人 = ☐

diǎn
点 丶

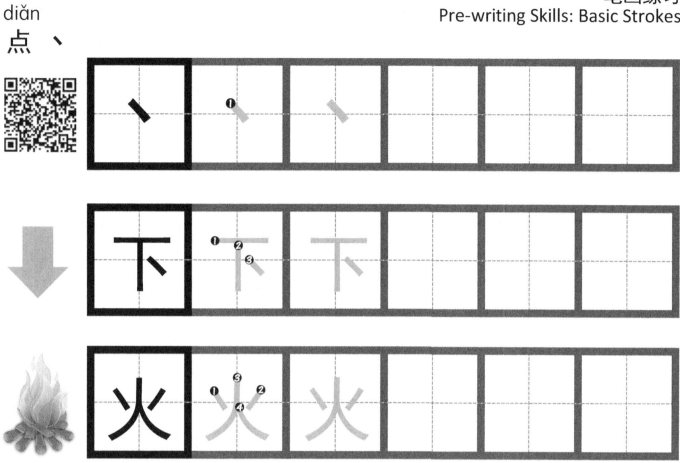

Trace all the 点 丶 you can find in each character. Then write down the number.

fāng	yǔ	chā	bèi	tóu
方	雨	叉	贝	头

| square | rain | fork | shell | head |

点 can be backward ヽ or forward ノ. Color the backward ヽ
^{lǜ} 绿色 and the forward ノ ^{zǐ} 紫色 in each character.
green   purple

xiǎo   xīn   shǎo

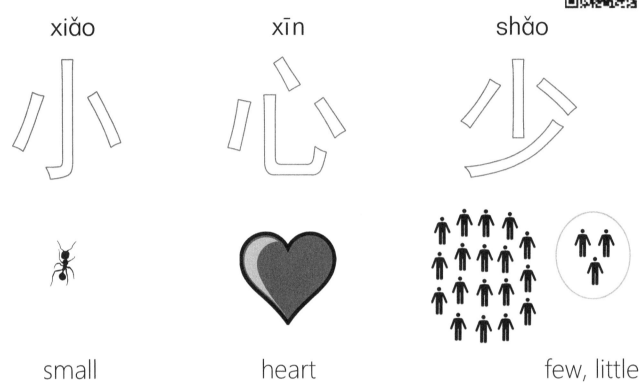

small   heart   few, little

What is missing? Add one stroke to complete each
character.

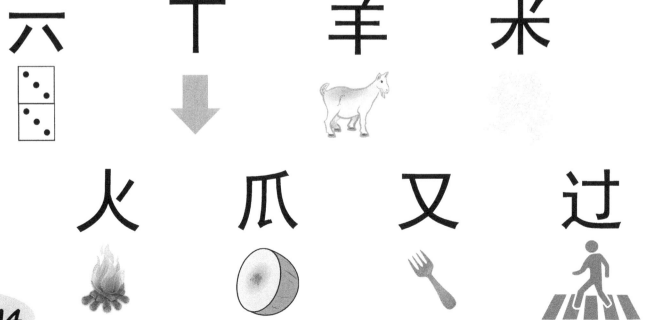

tí
提 ╱

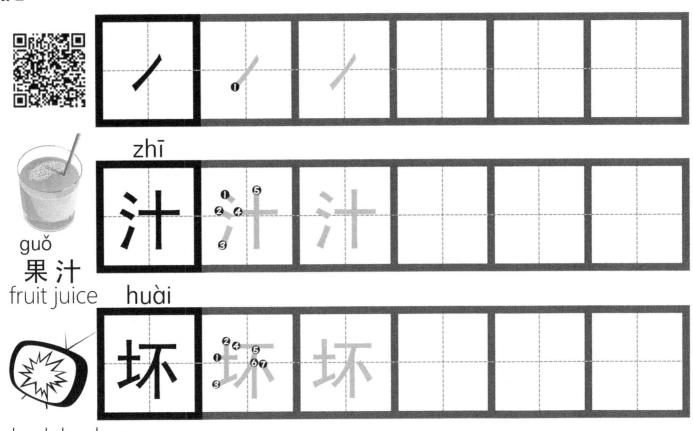

zhī
汁

guǒ
果汁
fruit juice

huài
坏

bad, broken

Find and trace 提 ╱ in these characters.

chóng	hàn	wán	dǎ
虫	汗	玩	打

insect, worm   sweat   play   beat, play, make

点、 or 提 ／ ? Color the 点、 黄色 (huáng) and the 提 ／ 橙色 (chéng)
in each character.
yellow   orange

lěng   hǎi

虫   冷   海

cold   ocean

Review. Name and write the six basic strokes in Chinese.

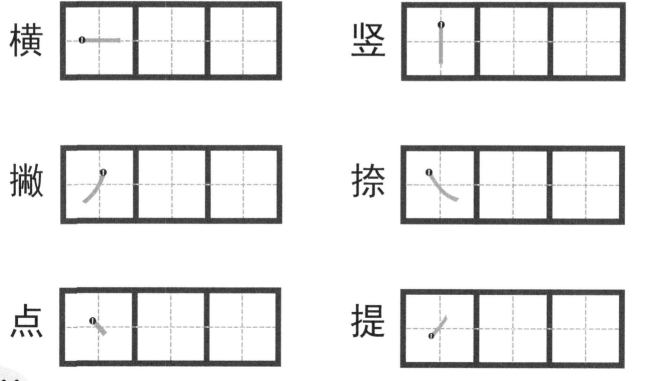

横   竖

撇   捺

点   提

16

Compound Strokes are made of two or more basic strokes. They are also called turning strokes because they make turns.

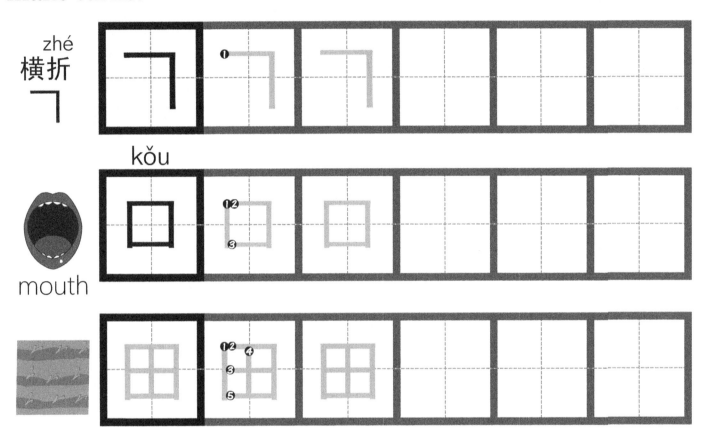

zhé
横折
⌐

kǒu
mouth

Find and trace 横折 ⌐ in these characters.

sì	wǔ	rì	zhōng	mǎ
四	五	日	中	马

| 4 | 5 | sun | middle | horse |

Read and color. Then circle the characters that have ㄱ.

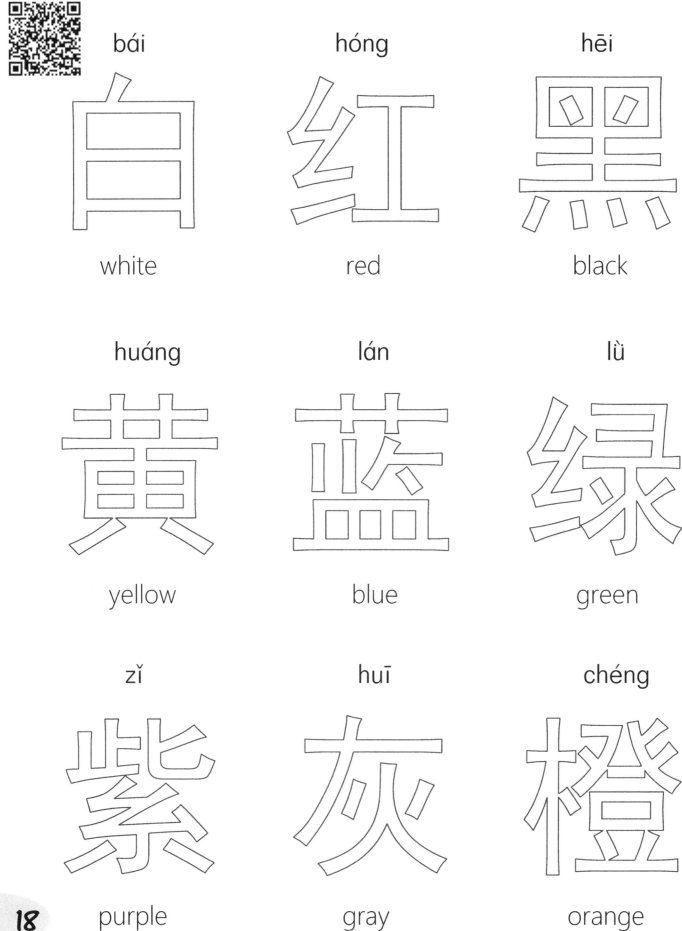

bái

white

hóng

red

hēi

black

huáng

yellow

lán

blue

lù

green

zǐ

purple

huī

gray

chéng

orange

18

gōu
横折钩 コ

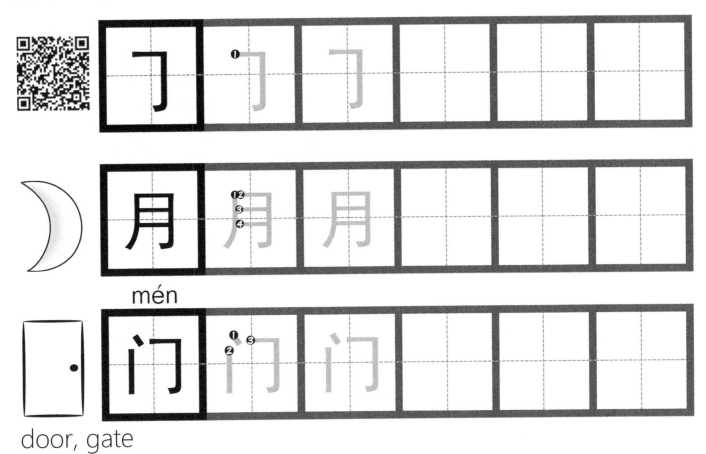

mén

door, gate

Find and trace 横折钩 コ in these characters.

jīn	dāo	sháo	wǎng	mǔ
巾	刀	勹	网	母

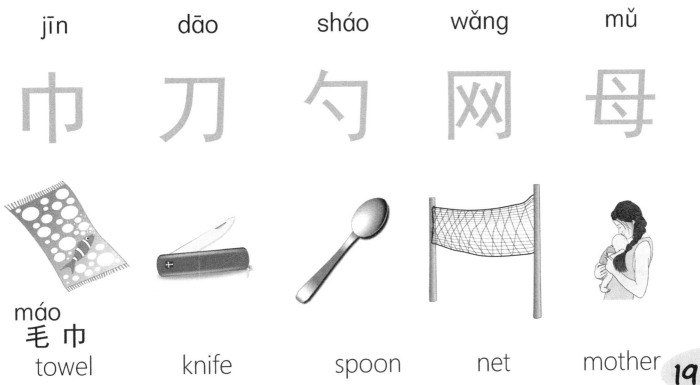

máo				
毛巾				
towel	knife	spoon	net	mother

19

Look, read, and match.

日

月

火

雨

竖折 ∟

shān

mountain

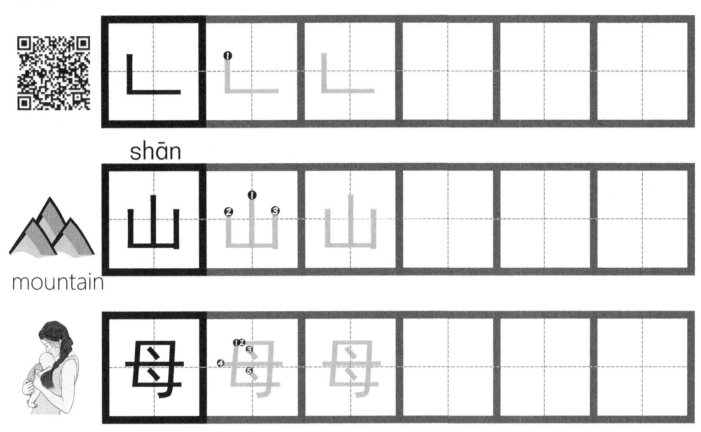

Circle all the ∟ you can find and then write down the number in Chinese.

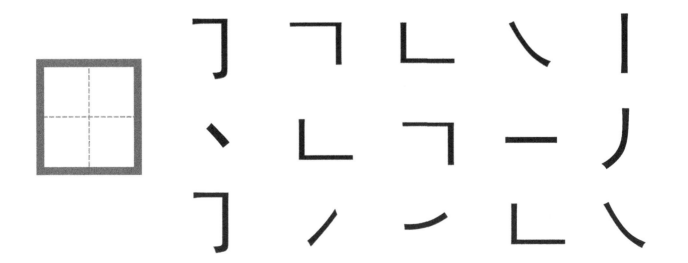

虫子*下山

Help the worms find their way down the hills.

出口

出口

山+山=出 (chū)

出口： exit

子*：originally meaning son or child, is now used as a
suffix for some one-character nouns. See Page 26 for more.

竖钩 亅

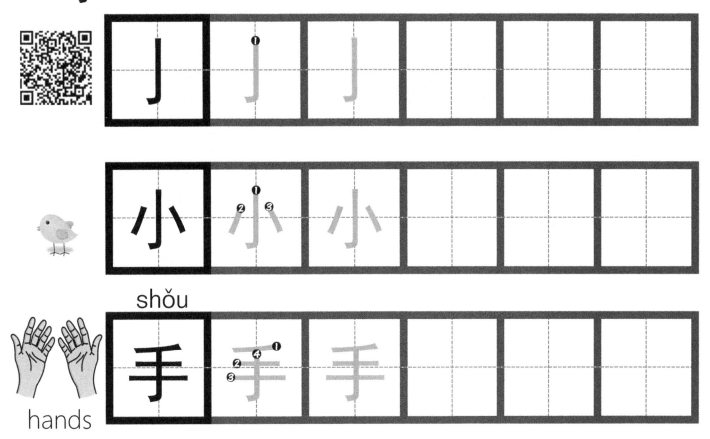

shǒu

hands

Find and trace 竖钩 亅 in these characters.

	qiú	shuǐ	yá	le
打	球	水	牙	了

打球
play ball

ball

water

teeth

hǎo
好了
done

Big or small? 哪 个 大 ，哪个 小 ？
nǎ gè
which one

24

横钩 ⁊

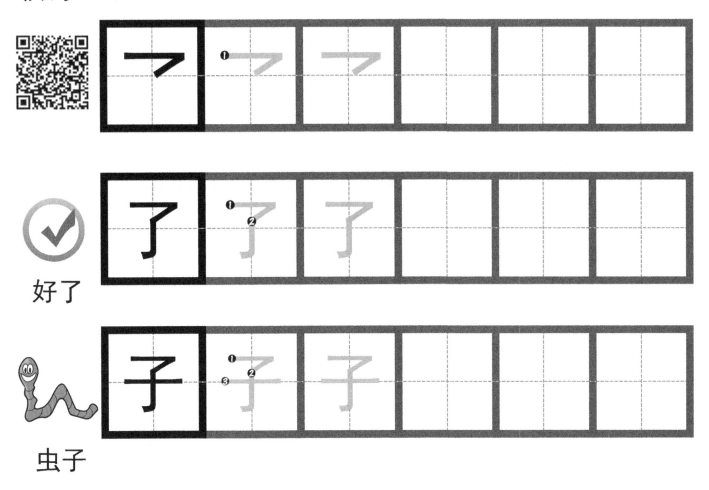

好了

虫子

Find and trace 横钩 ⁊ in these characters.

zǐ	pí	nǐ	jīn	chuī
籽	皮	你	今	吹

seed	skin	you	today	blow

Many words in Chinese end with 子. Can you use 子 to complete these words?

kuài

筷 [ ]

chopsticks

wà

袜 子

socks

jiǎo

饺 [ ]

dumplings

yè

叶 [ ]

leaf

mào

帽 [ ]

hat

tù

兔 [ ]

rabbit

fáng

房 [ ]

house

Do you know any other words that also end with 子?

横撇 フ

duō

多

many, much

Which character has the stroke? Circle it.

1. ㇇ 皮 水   2. ㇆ 月 日

3. ㇆ 门 口   4. フ 了 多

5. 亅 大 小   6. ㇖ 山 火

More or fewer? 哪个 多 ? 哪个 少 ?

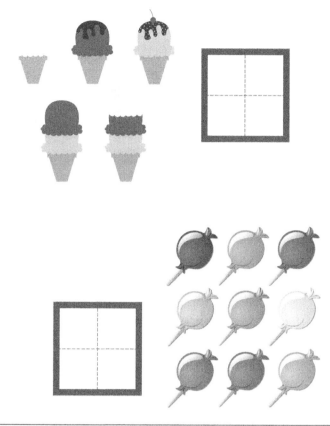

28

wān
竖弯钩 乚

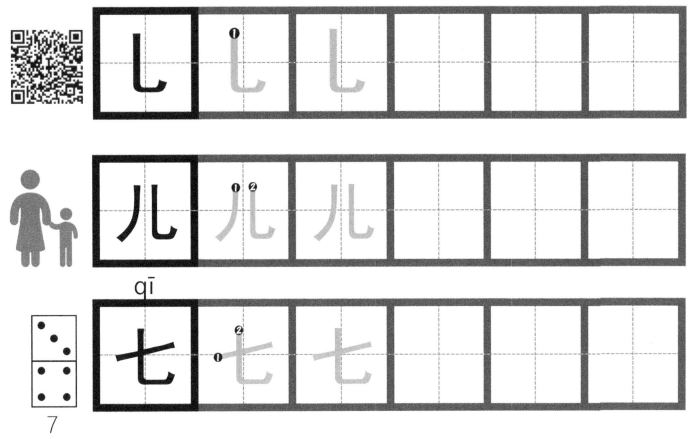

儿

qī
七

7

Find and trace 竖弯钩 乚 in these characters.

bà   tā   diàn   guāng

爸   他   电   光   兔

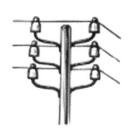

dad   he   electricity   light

Say the animals in Chinese. Circle the characters that have └. Then color the pictures.

hǔ

虎
tiger

兔

lóng

龙
dragon

马

shé

蛇
snake

牛

竖提 ∟

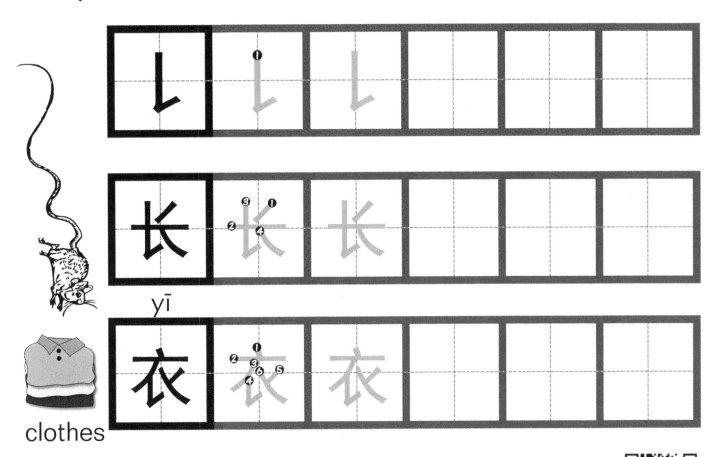

yī

clothes

Find and trace 竖提 ∟ in these characters.

nóng   mín   jiào   bǐ

农民   叫   比   瓜

5 > 3

5 比 3 大

farmer   call, shout   than

31

竖钩还是竖提？ 亅 or ㇄ ? Draw a line from the character to its matching umbrella.

小　瓜　水

hǎo

衣　球　好

长

good

竖折折钩 ㇉

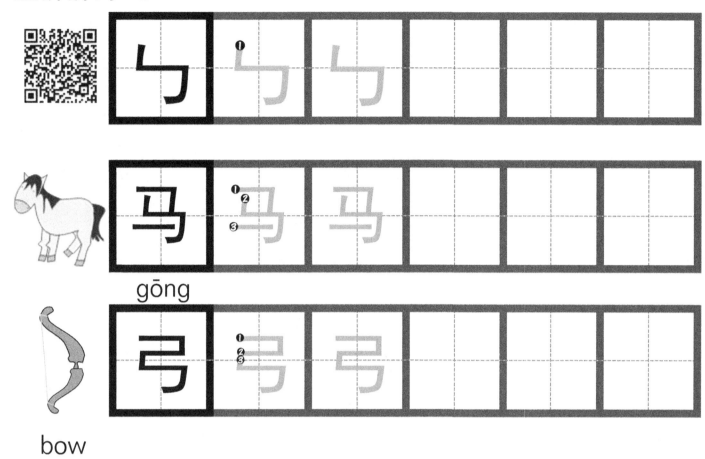

gōng

bow

Find and trace 竖折折钩 ㇉ in these characters.

| mā | xiě | dì | niǎo | hào |

| mom | write | younger brother | bird | 1. trumpet
2. number |

33

Can you help the boy find his missing ㄅ strokes? There are 8 of them.

撇折 乚

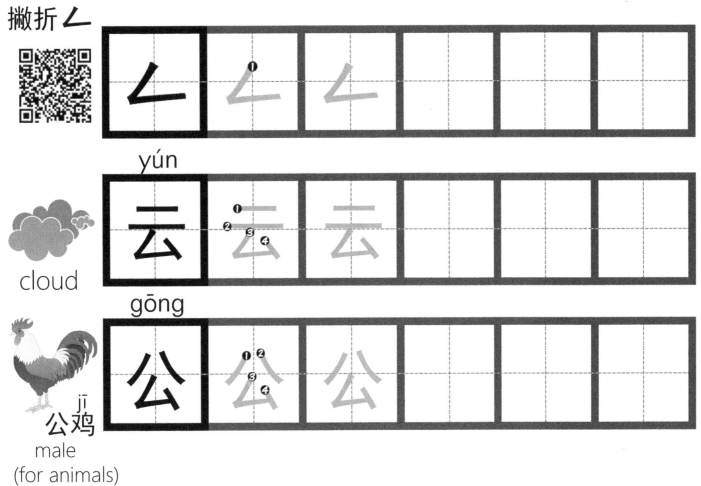

yún

cloud

gōng

jī
公鸡
male
(for animals)

Find and trace 撇折 乚 in these characters.

么　　车　　红　　去　　丢

qù　　diū

shén me
什 么
what

red　　　go　　throw

What do you see in this picture? Circle the characters.

天 月 云 山 水
鸟 马 火 田 雨

撇点 ㄑ

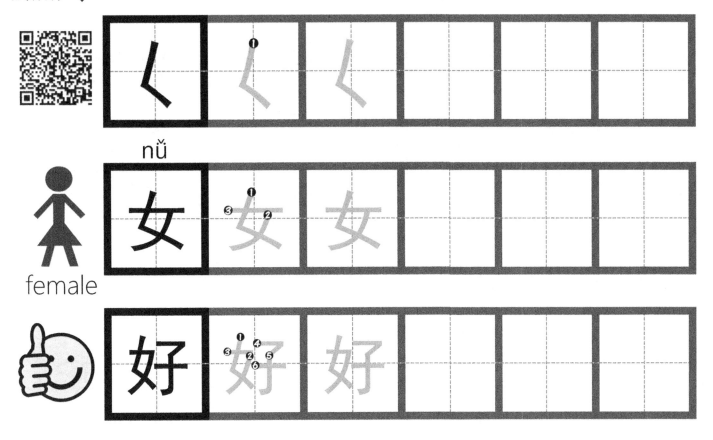

nǚ

female

女 means female. Find and trace 女 in these characters.

jiě	mèi	nǎi	tā
妈	姐	妹	奶	她

older sister   younger sister   grandma   she

How many people are there in your family? Circle the words for them and then draw a picture of your family.

爸爸　妈妈　哥哥　姐姐

older brother

弟弟　妹妹　爷爷　奶奶　我

grandpa   I

xié

斜钩/捺钩 乀

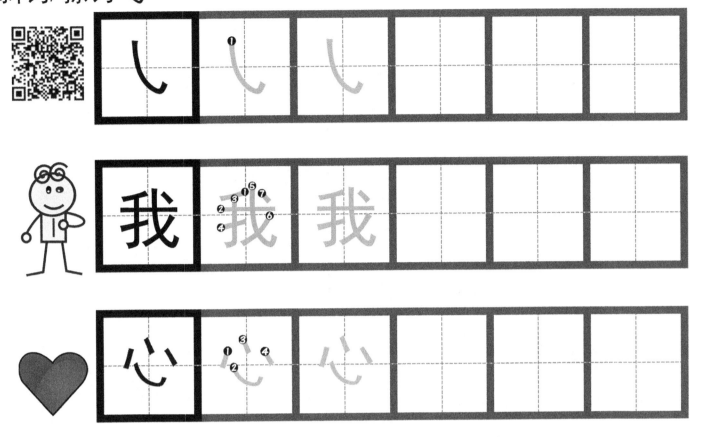

Look and match. Draw a line.

我

他

你

她

他<ruby>还<rt>hái</rt></ruby> <ruby>是<rt>shì</rt></ruby>她？ He or she? Use 亻 for a boy and 女 for a girl to complete the characters.

横斜钩 乀

fēi
fly

fēng
wind

横折弯钩 乁

jiǔ

jǐ

1. a few
2. how many

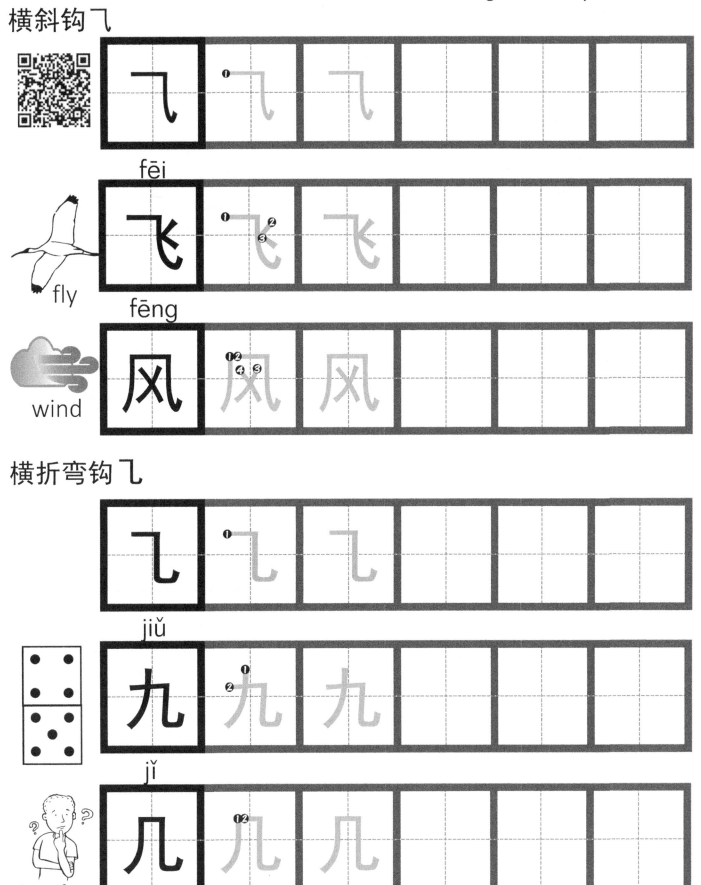

What can fly? Use to complete each word.

鸟

flying   bird

虫

jī

机

airplane

chuán

船

spaceship

wān
竖弯 乚

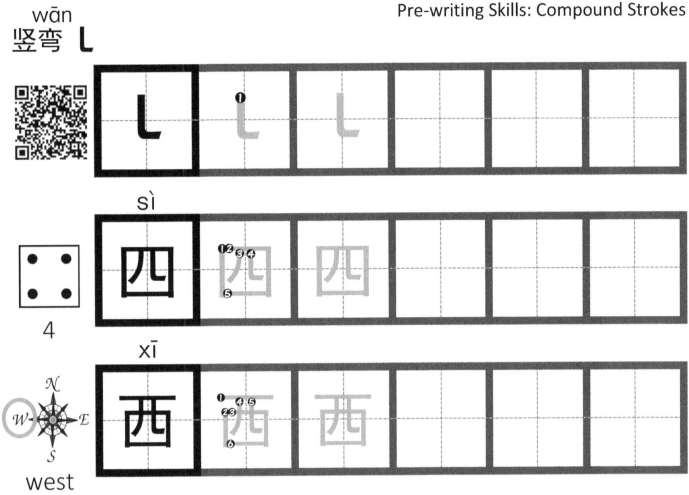

sì
四

4

xī
西

west

横折弯 乙

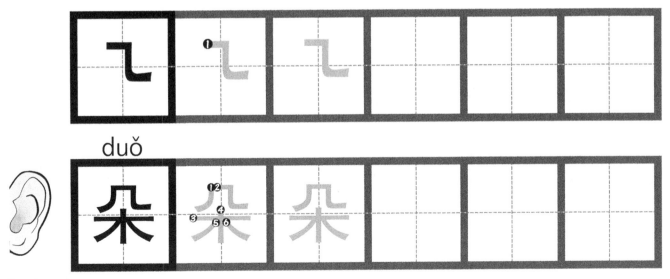

duǒ
朵

ěr duo
耳朵
ear

Write down the numbers in Chinese.

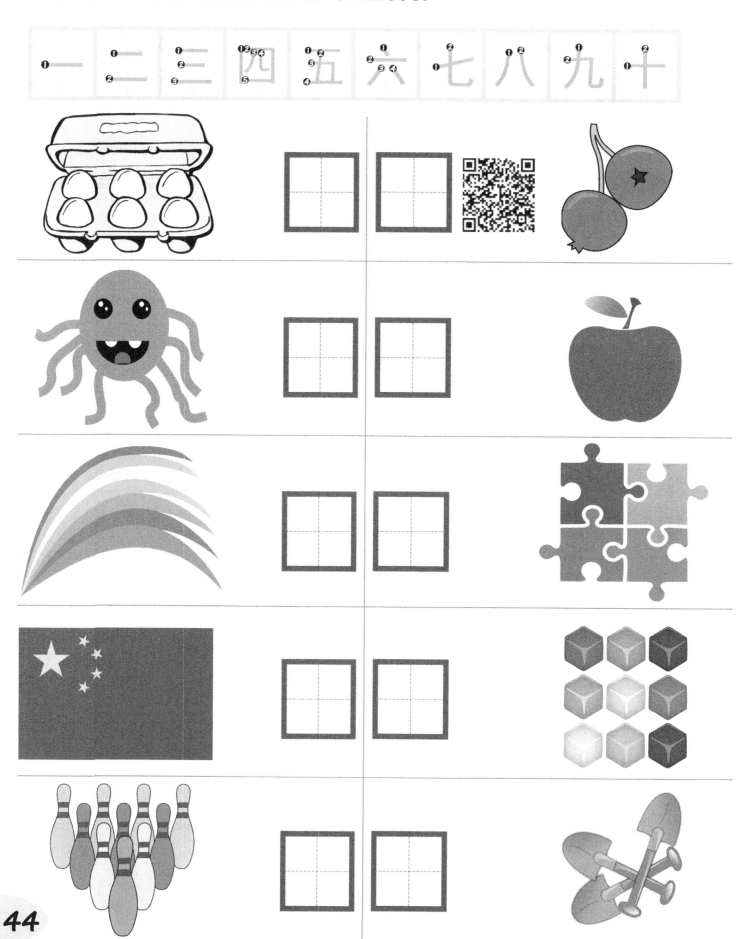

横折提 乚

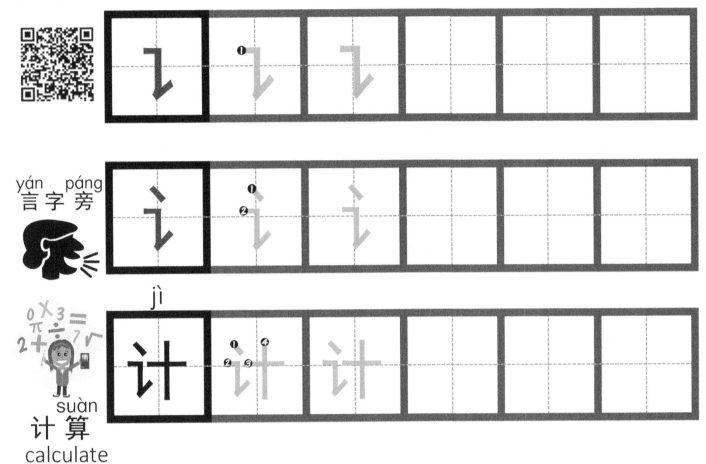

yán páng
言字旁

jì
suàn
计算
calculate

乚 is for speech. Find and trace 乚 in these characters.

qǐng   shuō   hàn yǔ   xiè

请   说   汉语   谢谢

Please

你好

Thank You

speak   Chinese (language)

横撇弯钩 乛

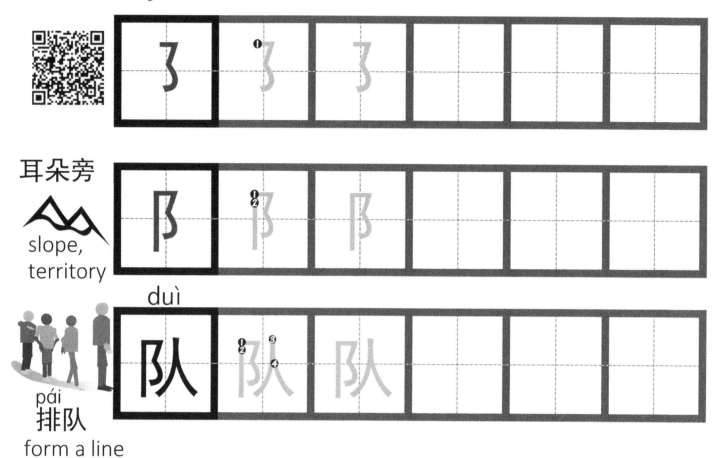

耳朵旁

slope, territory

duì

pái
排队
form a line

Find and trace 阝 in these characters.

yīn	yáng	nǎ	yóu
阴	阳	哪	邮

overcast

tài
太阳
sun

where, which

xiāng
邮 箱
mailbox

弯钩 ）

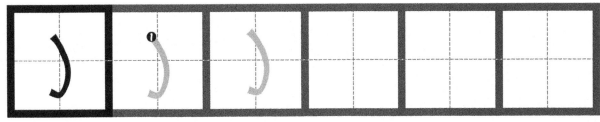

fǎnquǎn
反 犬 旁

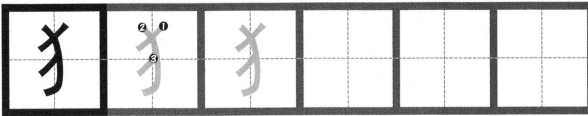

犭 is for animals that are dog-like. Say the word for each animal and trace the 犭. Then color the pictures.

gǒu 狗

māo 猫

hú li 狐狸

fox

hóu 猴

láng 狼

zhū 猪

monkey

wolf

pig

颜色和形状
Colors and Shapes

yán sè
颜色 Colors

Say the words with 红 and color the pictures.

píng guǒ
红苹果

huā
红花

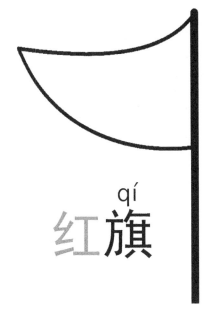

qí
红旗

dēng
红灯

红心

tài
红太阳

Say the words with 橙 and color the pictures.

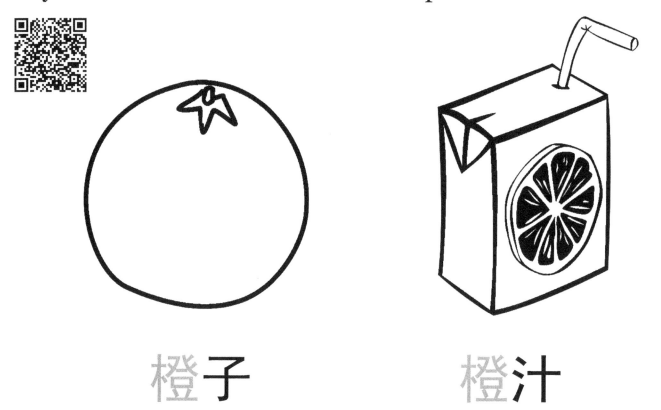

橙子   橙汁

Funny Vegetable names! Carrots are orange but they are not 橙萝卜. Cucumbers are green but they are not 绿瓜. Do you know their correct names?

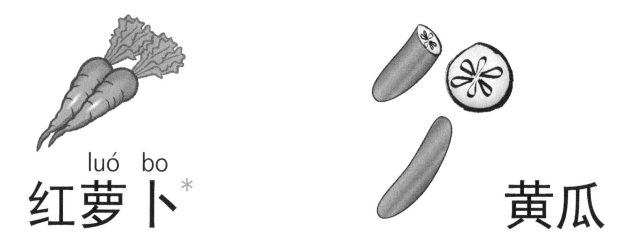

luó bo
红萝卜*

黄瓜

hú
*Carrots are also called 胡萝卜.

Say the words with 黄 and color the pictures.

黄鸟

黄梨
lí

yā
黄鸭

dòu
黄豆
soybean

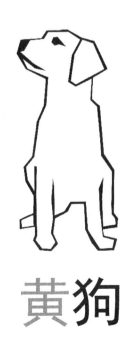

黄狗

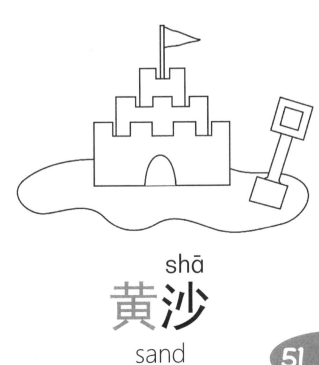

shā
黄沙
sand

51

Say the words with 绿 and color the pictures.

绿豆

绿叶

chá
绿茶
tea

shù
绿树
tree

cǎo
绿草
grass

Say the words with 蓝 and color the pictures.

méi
蓝莓

yǎn jing
蓝眼睛

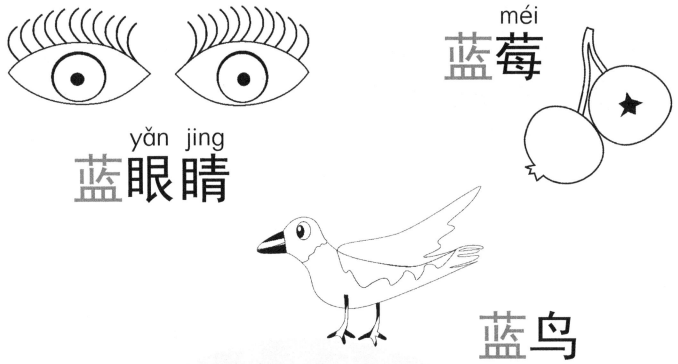

蓝鸟

蓝天

jīng
蓝鲸
whale

53

Say the words with 紫 and color the pictures.

pú táo
紫葡萄

qié
紫茄子
eggplant

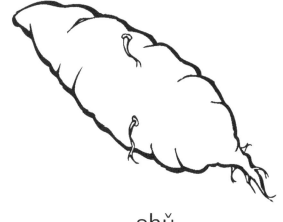

shǔ
紫薯
yam

yù
紫玉米

Say the words with zōng 棕 and color the pictures.

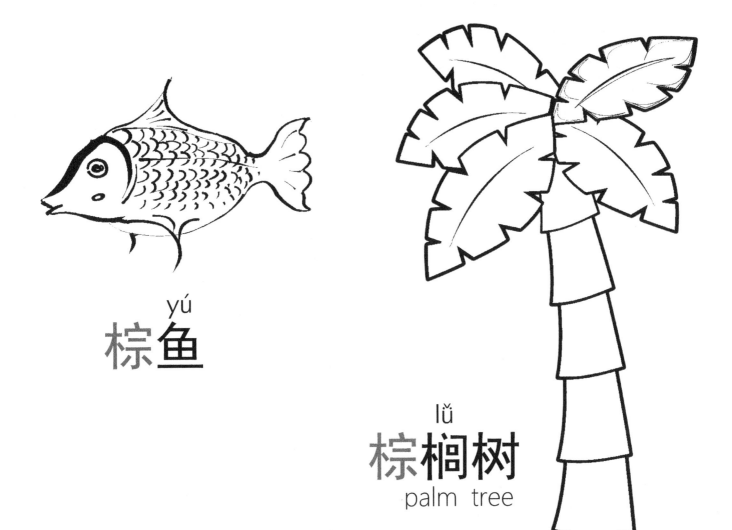

yú
棕**鱼**

lǔ
棕**榈树**
palm tree

xióng
棕**熊**

55

Say the words with 黑 and color the pictures.

黑眼睛

tóu fa
黑头发

bǎn
黑板
board

yè
黑夜
night

Say the words with 白 and match them with the correct pictures.

 白云

 白雪
xuě
snow

 白饭
fàn
rice

 白鹅
é
goose

 白天*

*白天 doesn't mean a white sky.
It means day time because it's bright during the day.

57

Say the words with 灰 and color the pictures.

小灰兔

大灰狼

lǘ
灰驴
donkey

shǔ
灰鼠

Color the lollipops!

xíng zhuàng
形 状 Shapes

Say the name of each shape and connect the dots.

yuán
圆形

zhèng
正方形

长方形

jiǎo
三角形

Read and match.

长方形

正方形

圆形

三角形

Say the name of each shape and connect the dots.

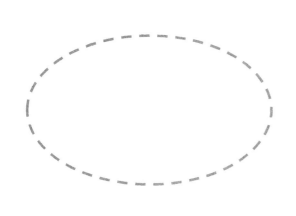

tuǒ
椭圆形

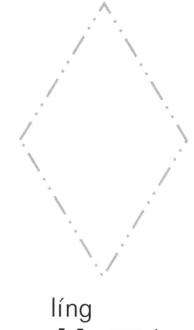

líng
菱形

心形

五角形

Read and match.

心形

五角形

菱形

椭圆形

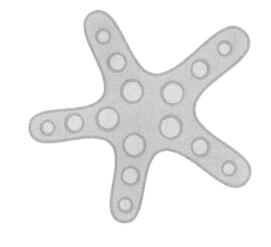

Color the Shapes.

正方形=蓝色　　　长方形=紫色　　　三角形=橙色　　椭圆形=灰色

圆形=红色　　　　心形=绿色　　　　五角形=黄色　　　菱形=棕色

Color the shapes any color you want.
Then cut them out and make a robot!

jī qì
机器人
robot

头=正方形　　耳朵=圆形

眼睛=心形　　头发=长方形

zuǐ ba
嘴巴=椭圆形　　手=菱形
mouth

牙=三角形

Glue here

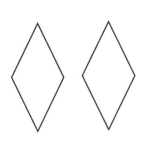
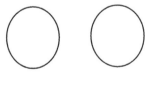

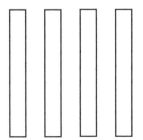

65

数字和日期
Numbers and Dates

shù zì
数字

Count and match.

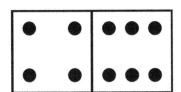

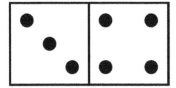

一
二
三
四
五
六
七
八
九
十

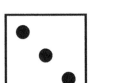

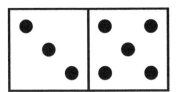

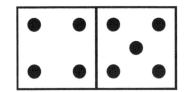

Circle groups of ten and write down the numbers in Chinese.

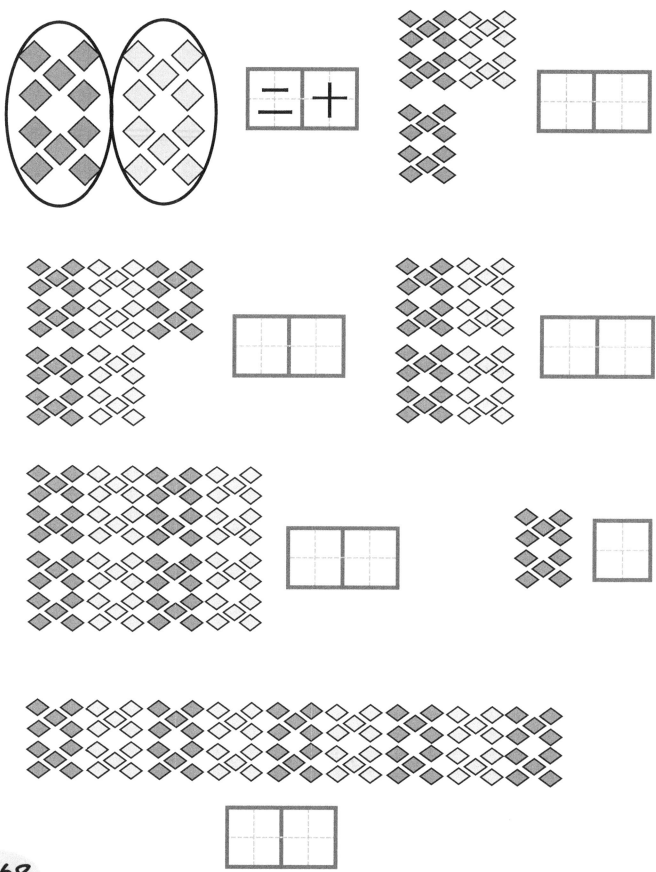

Fill in the missing numbers.

一		三		五		七	八		十
十一	十二		十四			十七		十九	二十
二十一		二十三		二十五	二十六			二十九	三十
三十一	三十二		三十四	三十五		三十七	三十八		四十
四十一		四十三	四十四		四十六			四十九	五十
	五十二		五十四		五十六	五十七			六十
六十一		六十三		六十五			六十八	六十九	
七十一	七十二			七十五	七十六		七十八		八十
		八十三			八十六	八十七		八十九	
	九十二		九十四			九十七		九十九	一百

Hundreds

bǎi

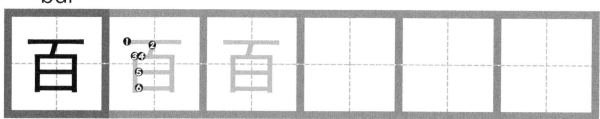

Can you write these numbers in Chinese?

351

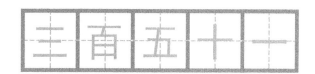

110

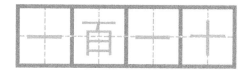

246

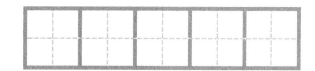

590

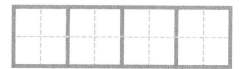

789

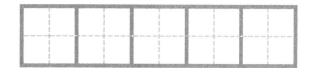

475

801

líng

909

Year and Age

nián

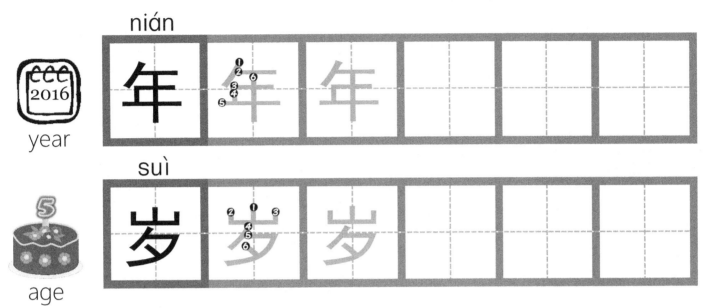

year

suì

age

In Chinese, we say years digit by digit, and then add 年 at the end. Read and write these years in Chinese.

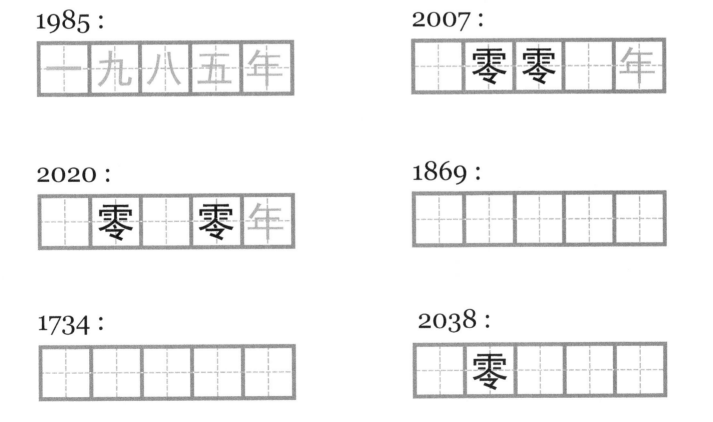

1985 : 一 九 八 五 年

2007 : 零 零 年

2020 : 零 零 年

1869 :

1734 :

2038 : 零

Challenge Question: What year is this year?

他/她几岁？ How old is he/she?

Look, count, and write.

他 ⬜⬜岁。

她 ⬜⬜。

他 ⬜⬜。

她 ⬜⬜。

Months

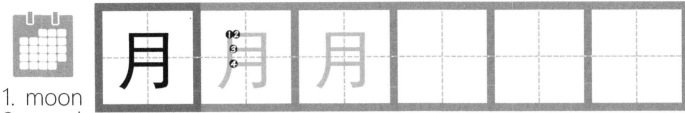

1. moon
2. month

Fill in the blanks.

一月
January

二□
February

March

四月
April

□月
May

六□
June

□月
July

八□
August

□月
September

□月
October

十一月
November

December

今天星期几？ xīng qī (week) What day (of the week) is today?

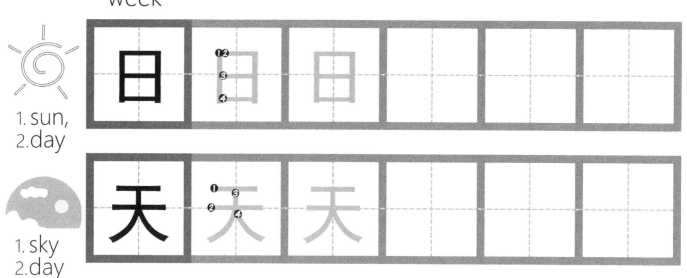

1. sun, 2. day

1. sky 2. day

Fill in the missing numbers and answer the question.

星期一
Monday

星期☐
Tuesday

星期三
Wednesday

星期☐
Thursday

星期五
Friday

星期☐
Saturday

星期天*
Sunday

今天星期几？

*Sunday is called 星期天 or 星期日.

日期 Dates

hào

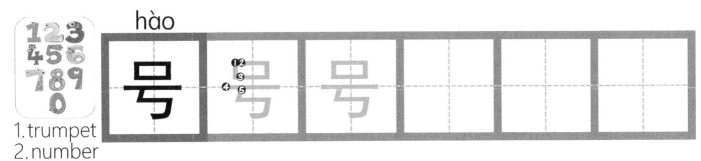

号 号 号

1. trumpet
2. number

Look at the calendar and write down the date.

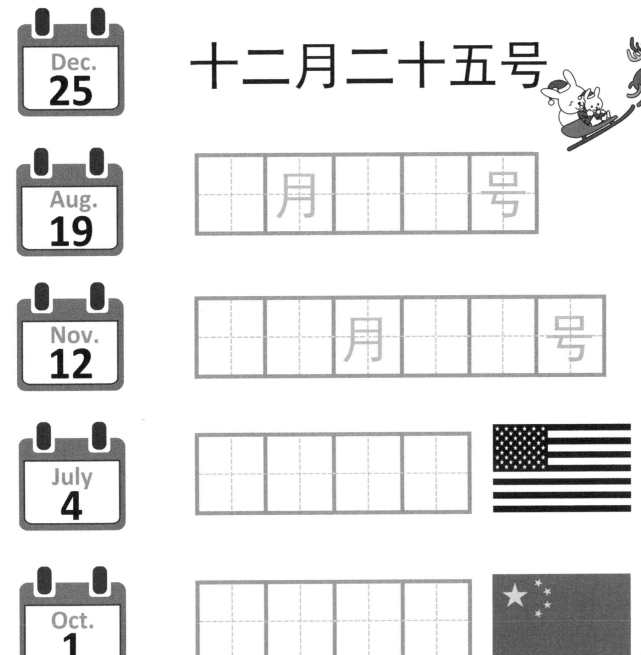

Dec. 25 — 十二月二十五号

Aug. 19 — 月 号

Nov. 12 — 月 号

July 4

Oct. 1

75

Read and match.

二零二五年
六月一号

二零三零年
十二月
二十九号

一九九零年
七月三十号

二零一七年
二月十四号

February 14, 2017

June 1, 2025

December 29, 2030

July 30, 1990

Fill in the blanks using the real date.

今天是几月几号？ What's the date today?

今天是 ⬚⬚ 月 ⬚⬚⬚ 号。

明天是几月几号？ What's the date tomorrow?

明天是 ⬚⬚ 月 ⬚⬚⬚ 号。

de shēng
你的 生 日是哪天？
your birthday

我的生日是 ⬚二⬚零⬚⬚⬚ 年
⬚⬚ 月 ⬚⬚⬚ 号。

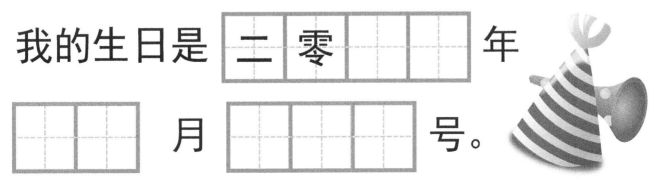

量词
Measure Words

Measure words help us count. There are hundreds of measure words in Chinese.

gè

个 is the most commonly used measure word. It is for individual things or people.

三个人

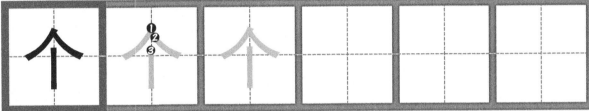

Read and draw.

一个太阳   一个月亮

79

Special Rule!

When used before a measure word, 二 becomes 两 (liǎng).

Practice writing 两 and complete the words with 两个.

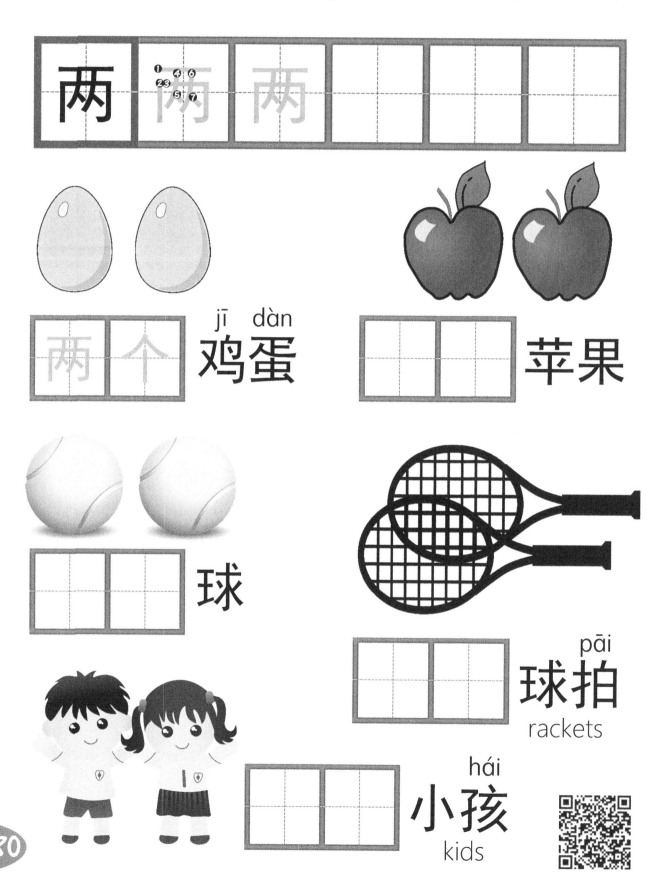

两　两　两

两个 鸡蛋 (jī dàn)

苹果

球

球拍 (pāi)
rackets

小孩 (hái)
kids

yǒu
有几个？ Count by 个 and fill in the blanks.

péng you
好朋友
friends

shū bāo
书 包

qì
气 球

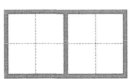

zhēng
风 筝

81

只 is generally used for small animals, but there are some exceptions like tigers and dinosaurs.

四只鸡

zhī

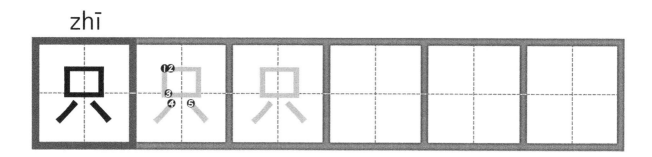

Read and draw.

三只小鸟

两只猫

有几只？ Count by 只 and write down the numbers.

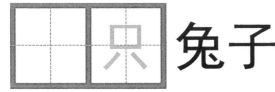 只 兔子

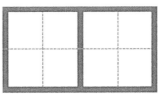 狐狸

lǎo
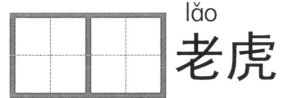 老虎

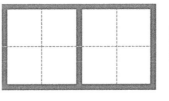 鸭子

只 is also for one in a pair.

一只手套
tào

Read and draw.

一只手

两只脚
jiǎo
foot

一只耳朵

两只眼睛

有几只？ Count by 只 and write down the numbers.

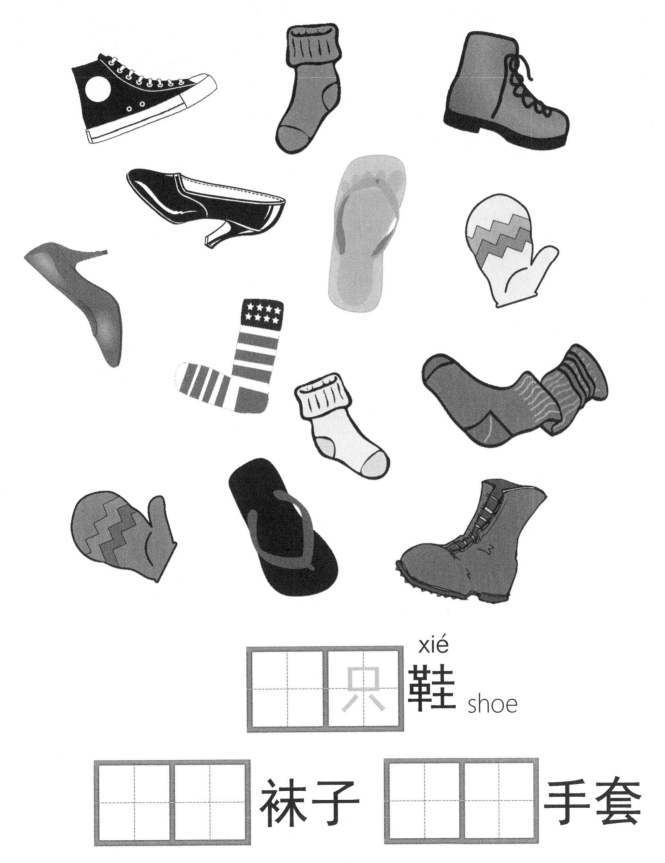

xié
☐ 只 鞋 shoe

☐ ☐ 袜子　☐ ☐ 手套

头 means head.

It is used to count big animals.

一头牛

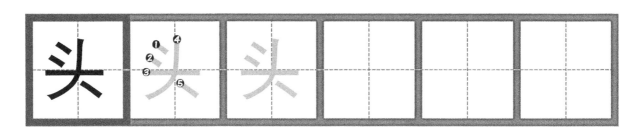

Read and draw.

两头猪

xiàng
一头大象
elephant

有几头？ Count by 头. Then read and match.

五头猪

两头大象

六头牛

shī
三头狮子
lion

条 is for animals that are thin and long .

一条鱼

tiáo

条	条	条			

Read and draw.

máo
两条毛毛虫
caterpillar

一条狗

有几条？ Count by 条 and fill in the blanks.

| | 条 鱼 | | 毛毛虫 |
| | 狗 | | 蛇 |

条 is also for things that are thin and long.
Read and match.

两条腿
tuǐ
leg

四条领带
lǐng dài
tie

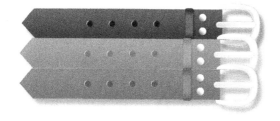

三条皮带
belt

一条胳膊
gē bo
arm

Horses are special! They have their own measure word 匹.

一匹马

pǐ

匹 匹 匹

有几匹？ Count by 匹 and write down the number.

匹马

Help the animals find their group.

只

条

93

块 is for chunks or thick pieces.

gāo
一块蛋糕

kuài

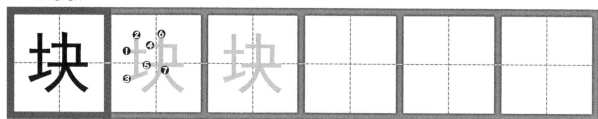

Read and draw.

qiǎo kè lì
一块巧克力
chocolate

xiàng
两块橡皮
eraser

有几块？ Count by 块. Then fill in the blanks.

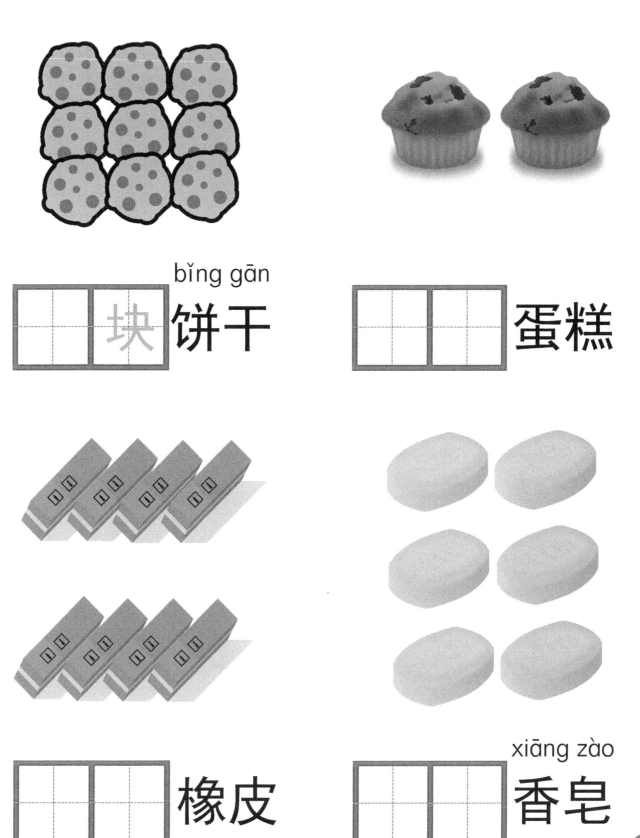

bǐng gān

| | 块 | 饼干 |

| | | 蛋糕 |

| | | 橡皮 |

xiāng zào

| | | 香皂 |
soap

95

张 is for flat and broad things.

zhǐ
一张纸

zhāng

Read and draw.

zhuō
一张桌子
table

chuáng
一张 床
bed

张 is also for face
and mouth.

liǎn
一张脸

zuǐ
一张嘴

Now read this little poem and try to extend it. Be careful
not to mess up with the measure words!

qīng wā
一只青蛙， 一张嘴，
frog
两只眼睛， 四条腿。

两只青蛙， □ 张 嘴，
□ 只 眼睛， □ 条 腿。

三只青蛙， □□□ 嘴，
□□ 眼睛， □□□ 腿。

97

双 means a pair of.

一双眼睛

shuāng

双 双 双

Read and draw.

一双鞋　　　　　两双袜子

只 or 双 ? One, or one pair?

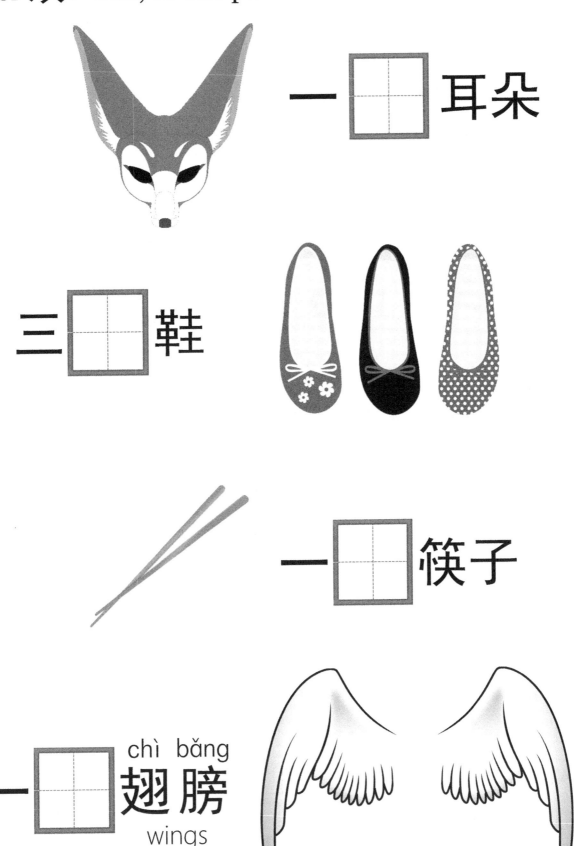

一 □ 耳朵

三 □ 鞋

一 □ 筷子

一 □ chì bǎng
翅 膀
wings

99

最常用字
Sight Words

shuí de jiā
谁*的家？ Whose home?

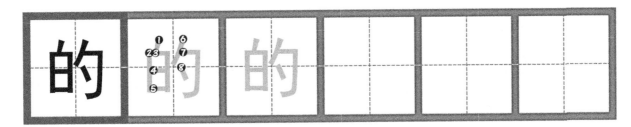

Read and match.

小狗的家

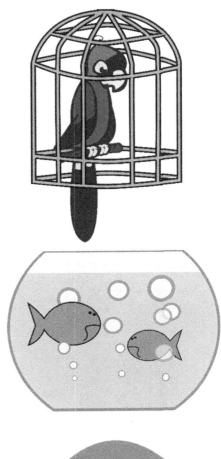

小鸟的家

小鱼的家

shuí
* 谁 is also pronounced as shéi.

谁的 ^{dōng xi} 东 西？ Whose stuff?

谁的 东 西？ Whose stuff?

Read and circle the correct answer.

1. 谁的雨^{sǎn}伞？

弟弟的　　妹妹的

2. 谁的风筝？

姐姐的　哥哥的

3. 谁的红萝卜？

小猫的　小兔子的

4. 谁的自^{zì xíng}行车？

他的　　她的

měi lì

美丽的家 A beautiful home. Read, match, and draw.

蓝蓝的   云

白白的   草

绿绿的   花

红红的   天

Read, trace, and circle.

1. 长长的鼻子 bí
nose

2. 圆圆的脸

3. 尖尖的牙齿 jiān chǐ
sharp   teeth

4. 高高的个子 gāo
tall   stature

méi
有没有？ Do you have or no?

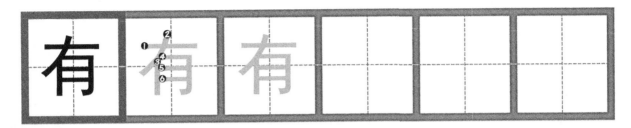

Read and trace.

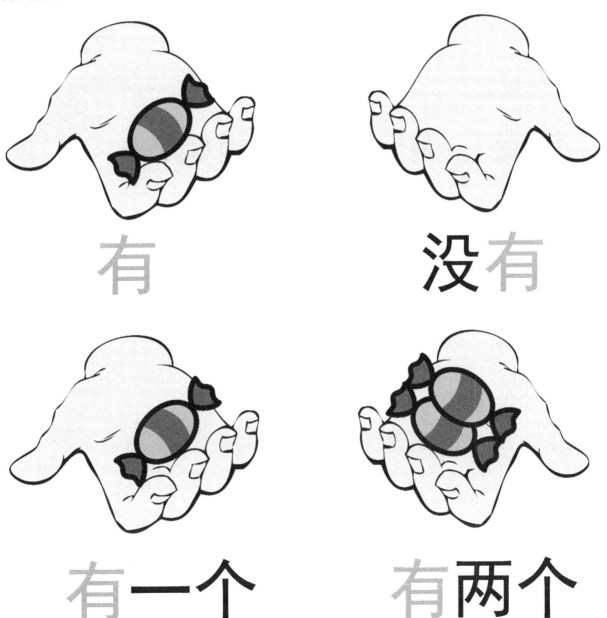

有   没有

有一个   有两个

Circle the correct answers and fill in the blanks.

你有没有哥哥/姐姐/弟弟/妹妹？
有几个？

我　没有　有 □ 个　哥哥，

没有　有 □ 个　姐姐，

没有　有 □ 个　弟弟，

没有　有 □ 个　妹妹。

Color, cut and paste.

天上有

dì
地上有
on the ground

lǐ
水里有
in

Read and circle.

我家有

电视
shì

自行车

球

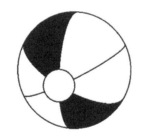

狗

猫

鸡

Fill in the blanks with the words in the boxes.

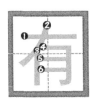 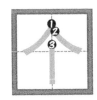 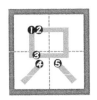

1. 书包里有什么？

有一 ⬜ 猫。

2. 树上有什么？

⬜ 五 ⬜ 苹果。

3. 水里有什么？

⬜ 三 ⬜ 鱼。

Read and draw.

guài wu
大怪物
monster

圆圆的脸

尖尖的牙齿

有三只眼睛

有四个耳朵

有五只手

没有鼻子

没有头发

wěi ba
有两条尾巴

兔子在哪里？ Where is the rabbit?

zài

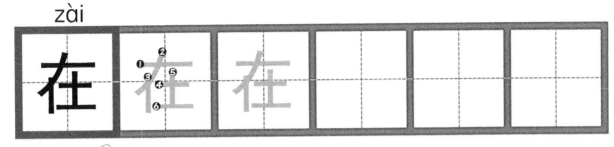

mào　　　miàn
在帽子上 面

lǐ
在…里面

在…下面

qián
在…前面

在…后面

pángbiān
在…旁边

Read each question and circle the correct answer.

小猫在哪里？

在书包 后面 里面

弟弟在哪里？

在桌子 下面 旁边

小鸟在哪里？

在电视 前面 上面

Read and color.

一二三四五六七，

我的朋友在哪里？

xué xiào
在学校，在家里。
school

zhè
我的朋友在这里。
here

113

他/她在做什么？ What is he/she doing?

zuò

Read, trace, and match.

她在画画。
huà
draw, paint

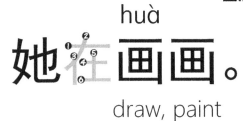

他在唱歌。
chàng gē
sing a song

她在玩球。

他在骑车。
qí
ride a bike

Read and color.

wá
两个小娃娃，
little kid

zhèng huà
正在打电话。
phone call

wèi ya
喂喂喂，你在哪里呀？
Hey

āi yòu yuán
哎哎哎，我在幼儿园。
Ah   pre-school

你在做什么？

xué
我在学唱歌。
learn

115

Read and match.

 在地上 游 yóu swim

 在水里 飞

 在天上 爬 pá climb

 在树上 跑 pǎo

了 indicates change.

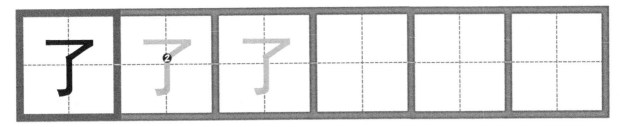

Read, trace, and color.

qiū
秋天
fall (season)

lái
来 了
come

天气
weather

liáng
凉 了
cool

树叶

黄 了

树叶

luò
落 了
drop

117

Feelings. Our feelings change from time to time. Use to complete these words.

kū

哭 了

crying

xiào

笑

smiling

kùn

困

sleepy

lèi

累

tired

è

饿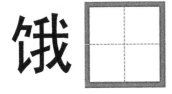

hungry

kě

渴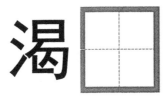

thirsty

rè

热

hot

lěng

冷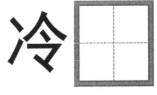

cold

119

Read and match.

下雨了

下雪了

出来了

跑走了

不　No/not

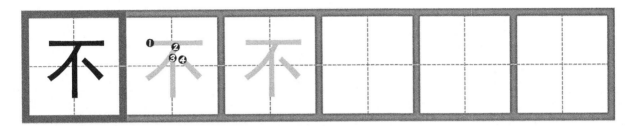

开心 　　不开心

Read and draw.

个子高　个子不高　　　雨大　雨不大

Read, write, and match.

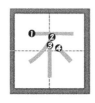 多

冷

长

圆

哭

zhè
这是 This is...

shì

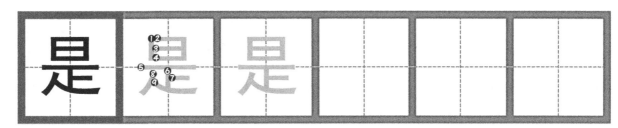

这是我的家。

Read and draw.

这是我。

这不是我。

123

Read and circle the correct picture.

1. 这是一只小鸟。

2. 这是两条鱼。

3. 这是我的书包。

4. 这不是校<ruby>车<rt>xiào</rt></ruby>。
school bus

5. 这不是爸爸的鞋。

吗 yes-no question marker

ma

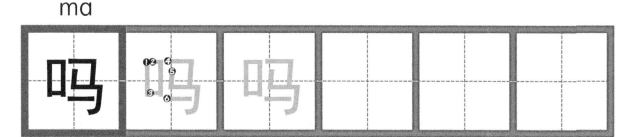

 你好吗？

 我很好，
hěn
very
谢谢！

Read and circle the correct answer.

1. 你是女孩吗？ 　　是　　不是

2. 你家有狗吗？ 　　有　　没有

3. 你妈妈在家吗？ 　　在　　不在

ài chī
4. 你爱吃<u>鱼</u>吗？ 　　爱　　不爱
love to eat

Complete each question with 吗 and circle your answer.

kǎ
小卡车好玩 吗 ？ 好玩
truck fun   不好玩

饺子好吃 ☐ ？ 好吃
yummy   不好吃

你爱唱歌 ☐ ？ 爱
                     不爱

shuì jiào
这只小猫在睡 觉 ☐ ？ 在
sleep   不在

你会做什么？ What can you do?

huì

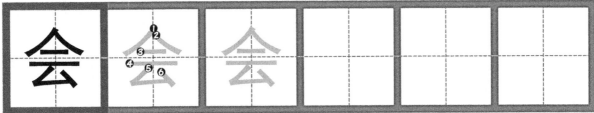

Read and circle ✓ or ✗.

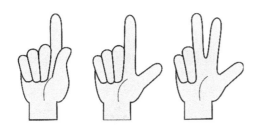

shǔ shù
我会数数。 ✓ ✗
count

我会画画。 ✓ ✗

我会打电话。 ✓ ✗

míng zi
我会写名字。 ✓ ✗
name

127

Complete the sentences with 会 or 不会.

 我 □□ 骑自行车。

 我 □□ <ruby>拍<rt>pāi</rt></ruby>球。
bounce

 我 □□ 唱中<ruby>文<rt>wén</rt></ruby>歌。
Chinese

 我 □□ 游<ruby>泳<rt>yǒng</rt></ruby>。

 我 □□ <ruby>用<rt>yòng</rt></ruby>筷子。
use

Read and match.

会下蛋

wāng
会汪汪叫
woof

guāng
会发光
glow

会爬树

bǎ
把门打开 Open the door.

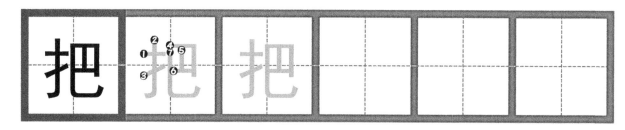

把 门打开

yī fu chuān
衣服穿上*
put on

wán
苹果吃完
finish

*穿上：to put on clothes, socks, and shoes.

Read and match.

bì
把眼睛闭上
close

hé
把盒子打开
box

dài
把帽子戴上*
put on

把袜子穿上

*戴上：to put on accessories (hat, watch, glasses, etc.)

和 ...and...

hé

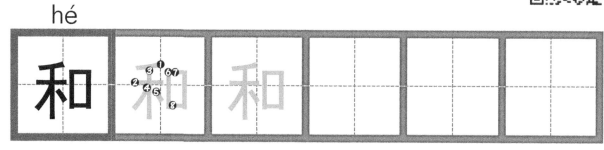

 苹果和橙子

Read and draw.

miàn bāo

面包和牛奶

bread   milk

我和朋友

Read, write, and match.

姐姐  妹妹

哥哥 ☐ 弟弟

shǔ

猫 ☐ 老鼠

wū guī

兔子 ☐ 乌龟
turtle

133

答案
Answers

（For questions not included, answers may vary.）

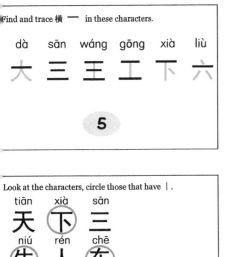

Find and trace 横 一 in these characters.

dà　sān　wáng　gōng　xià　liù

大　三　王　工　下　六

5

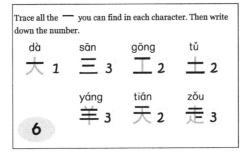

Trace all the 一 you can find in each character. Then write down the number.

dà　　sān　　gōng　　tǔ

大 1　三 3　工 2　土 2

yáng　　tiān　　zǒu

羊 3　天 2　走 3

6

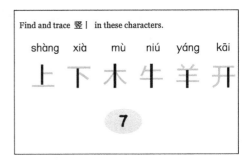

Find and trace 竖 丨 in these characters.

shàng　xià　mù　niú　yáng　kāi

上　下　木　牛　羊　开

7

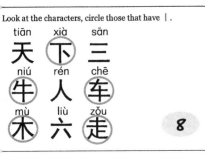

Look at the characters, circle those that have 丨.

tiān　xià　sān

天　下　三

niú　rén　chē

牛　人　车

mù　liù　zǒu

木　六　走

8

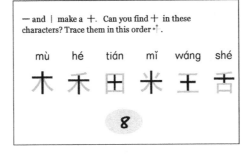

一 and 丨 make a 十. Can you find 十 in these characters? Trace them in this order 一丨.

mù　hé　tián　mǐ　wáng　shé

木　禾　田　米　王　舌

8

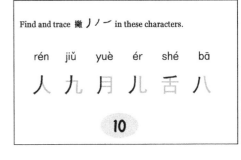

Find and trace 撇 丿 一 in these characters.

rén　jiǔ　yuè　ér　shé　bā

人　九　月　儿　舌　八

10

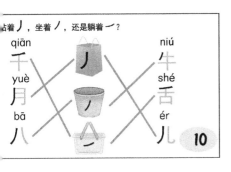

站着 丿，坐着 丿，还是躺着 一？

qiān
千
yuè
月
bā
八

niú
牛
shé
舌
ér
儿

10

Find and trace 捺 乀 in these characters.

mù　huǒ　cháng　guā　bā　tiān

木　火　长　瓜　八　天

11

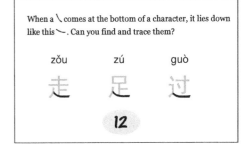

When a 乀 comes at the bottom of a character, it lies down like this ㇏. Can you find and trace them?

zǒu　　zú　　guò

走　足　过

12

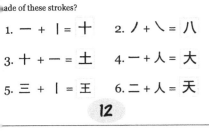

Stroke additions. Can you write down a character that is made of these strokes?

1. 一 + 丨 = 十　　2. 丿 + 乀 = 八

3. 十 + 一 = 土　　4. 一 + 人 = 大

5. 三 + 丨 = 王　　6. 二 + 人 = 天

12

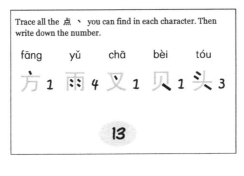

Trace all the 点 丶 you can find in each character. Then write down the number.

fāng　　yǔ　　chā　　bèi　　tóu

方 1　雨 4　叉 1　贝 1　头 3

13

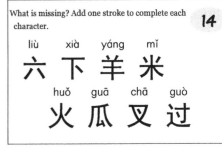

What is missing? Add one stroke to complete each character.

14

liù　xià　yáng　mǐ

六　下　羊　米

huǒ　guā　chā　guò

火　瓜　叉　过

Find and trace 提 ㇀ in these characters.

chóng　hàn　wán　dǎ

虫　汗　玩　打

15

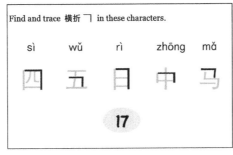

Find and trace 横折 ㄱ in these characters.

sì　wǔ　rì　zhōng　mǎ

四　五　日　中　马

17

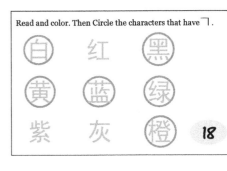

Read and color. Then Circle the characters that have ㄱ.

白　红　黑

黄　蓝　绿

紫　灰　橙　18

Find and trace 横折钩 ㇆ in these characters.

jīn　dāo　sháo　wǎng　mǔ

巾　刀　勺　网　母

19

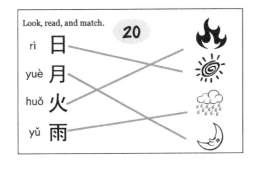

Look, read, and match.　20

rì 日
yuè 月
huǒ 火
yǔ 雨

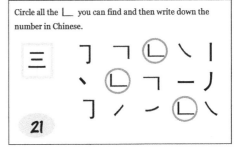

Circle all the 乚 you can find and then write down the number in Chinese.

21

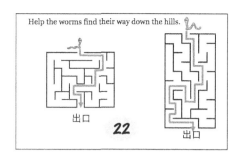

Help the worms find their way down the hills.

出口
出口

22

Find and trace 竖钩 亅 in these characters.

dǎ	qiú	shuǐ	yá	le
打	球	水	牙	了

23

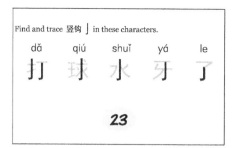

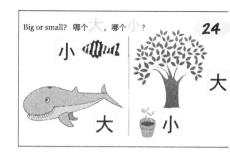

Big or small? 哪个大，哪个小？

小
大
大
小

24

小
小
大
大

24

Find and trace 横钩 乛 in these characters.

zǐ	pí	nǐ	jīn	chuī
籽	皮	你	今	吹

25

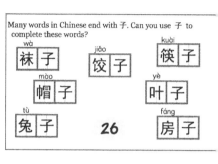

Many words in Chinese end with 子. Can you use 子 to complete these words?

wà 袜子　jiǎo 饺子　kuài 筷子

mào 帽子　yè 叶子

tù 兔子　fáng 房子

26

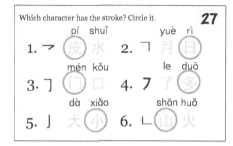

Which character has the stroke? Circle it.

1. 乛 pí 皮 shuǐ 水　2. ㇆ yuè 月 rì 日

3. ㇆ mén 门 kǒu 口　4. ㇇ le 了 duō 多

5. 亅 dà 大 xiǎo 小　6. ㇄ shān 山 huǒ 火

27

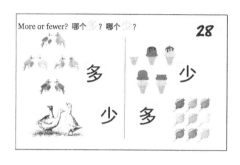

More or fewer? 哪个多？哪个少？

多
少
少
多

28

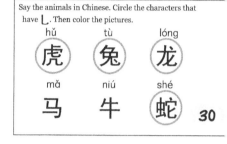

Say the animals in Chinese. Circle the characters that have ㇄. Then color the pictures.

hǔ	tù	lóng
虎	兔	龙
mǎ	**niú**	**shé**
马	牛	蛇

30

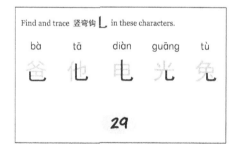

Find and trace 竖弯钩 乚 in these characters.

bà	tā	diàn	guāng	tù
爸	他	电	光	兔

29

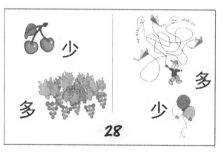

少
多
多
少

28

Find and trace 竖提 𠄌 in these characters.

nóng mín	jiào	bǐ	guā
农民	叫	比	瓜

31

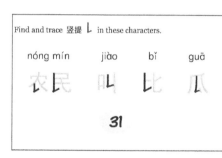

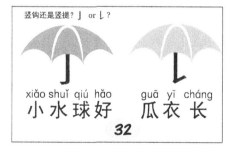

竖钩还是竖提？亅 or 𠄌？

xiǎo shuǐ qiú hǎo　guā yī cháng

小水球好　瓜衣长

32

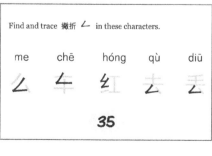

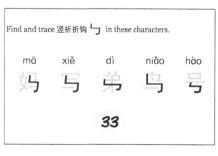

Find and trace 竖折折钩 ㄣ in these characters.

mā	xiě	dì	niǎo	hào
妈	写	弟	鸟	号

33

Can you help the boy find his missing ㄣ strokes? There are 8 of them.

34

Find and trace 撇折 𠃋 in these characters.

me	chē	hóng	qù	diū
么	车	红	去	丢

35

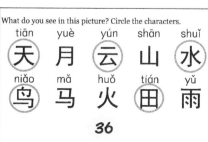

What do you see in this picture? Circle the characters.

tiān	yuè	yún	shān	shuǐ
天	月	云	山	水
niǎo	**mǎ**	**huǒ**	**tián**	**yǔ**
鸟	马	火	田	雨

36

女 means female. Find and trace 女 in these characters.

mā	jiě	mèi	nǎi	tā
妈	姐	妹	奶	她

37

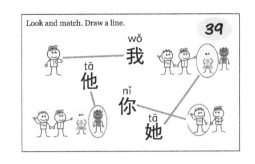

Look and match. Draw a line.

wǒ 我
tā 他
nǐ 你
tā 她

39

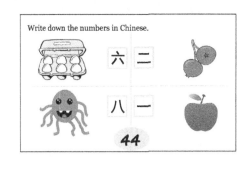

Write down the numbers in Chinese.

六 二
八 一

44

What can fly? Use 飞 to complete each word.

fēi niǎo	chóng
飞 鸟	飞 虫

jī	chuán
飞 机	飞 船

42

他还是她？ He or she? Use 亻 for a boy and 女 for a girl to complete the characters.

她 他
她 他
他 她

40

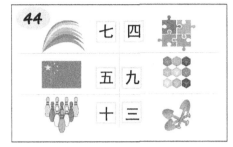

44

七 四
五 九
十 三

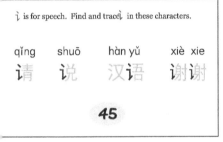

讠 is for speech. Find and trace 讠 in these characters.

qǐng	shuō	hàn yǔ	xiè xie
请	说	汉语	谢谢

45

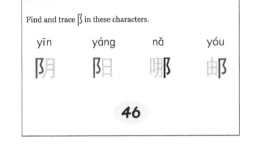

Find and trace 阝 in these characters.

yīn	yáng	nǎ	yóu
阴	阳	哪	邮

46

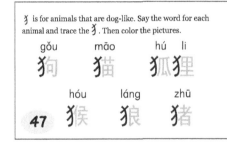

犭 is for animals that are dog-like. Say the word for each animal and trace the 犭. Then color the pictures.

gǒu	māo	hú li
狗	猫	狐狸

hóu	láng	zhū
猴	狼	猪

47

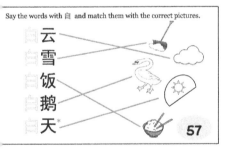

Say the words with 白 and match them with the correct pictures.

白 云
白 雪
白 饭
白 鹅
白 天

57

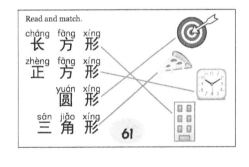

Read and match.

cháng fāng xíng 长 方 形
zhèng fāng xíng 正 方 形
yuán xíng 圆 形
sān jiǎo xíng 三 角 形

61

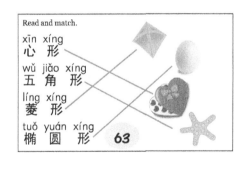

Read and match.

xīn xíng 心 形
wǔ jiǎo xíng 五 角 形
líng xíng 菱 形
tuǒ yuán xíng 椭 圆 形

63

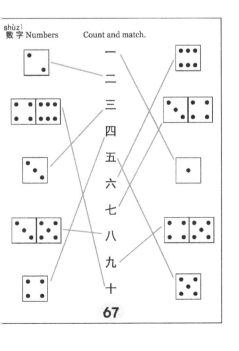

shùzì
数字 Numbers   Count and match.

一
二
三
四
五
六
七
八
九
十

67

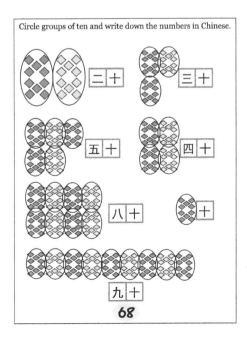

Circle groups of ten and write down the numbers in Chinese.

二十
三十
五十
四十
八十
十
九十

68

Numbers 1-100
Fill in the missing numbers in Chinese.

一	二	三	四	五	六	七	八	九	十
一	二	三	四	五	六	七	八	九	十
十一	十二	十三	十四	十五	十六	十七	十八	十九	二十
二十一	二十二	二十三	二十四	二十五	二十六	二十七	二十八	二十九	三十
三十一	三十二	三十三	三十四	三十五	三十六	三十七	三十八	三十九	四十
四十一	四十二	四十三	四十四	四十五	四十六	四十七	四十八	四十九	五十
五十一	五十二	五十三	五十四	五十五	五十六	五十七	五十八	五十九	六十
六十一	六十二	六十三	六十四	六十五	六十六	六十七	六十八	六十九	七十
七十一	七十二	七十三	七十四	七十五	七十六	七十七	七十八	七十九	八十
八十一	八十二	八十三	八十四	八十五	八十六	八十七	八十八	八十九	九十
九十一	九十二	九十三	九十四	九十五	九十六	九十七	九十八	九十九	一百

69

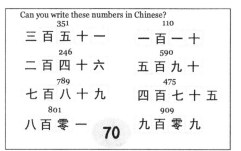

Can you write these numbers in Chinese?

351 三百五十一
110 一百一十
246 二百四十六
590 五百九十
789 七百八十九
475 四百七十五
801 八百零一
909 九百零九

70

Read and write these years in Chinese.

71

1985: 一九八五年
2007: 二零零七年
2020: 二零二零年
1869: 一八六九年
1734: 一七三四年
2038: 二零三八年

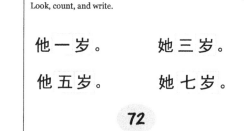

Look, count, and write.

他一岁。　她三岁。

他五岁。　她七岁。

72

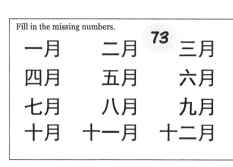

Fill in the missing numbers.

73

一月　二月　三月
四月　五月　六月
七月　八月　九月
十月　十一月　十二月

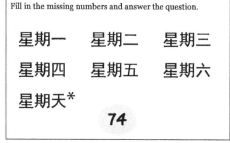

Fill in the missing numbers and answer the question.

星期一　星期二　星期三
星期四　星期五　星期六
星期天*

74

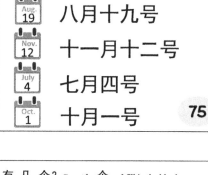

Aug. 19　八月十九号
Nov. 12　十一月十二号
July 4　七月四号
Oct. 1　十月一号

75

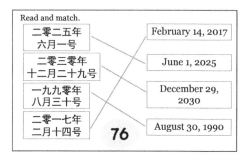

Read and match.

二零二五年 六月一号 — June 1, 2025
二零三零年 十二月二十九号 — December 29, 2030
一九九零年 八月三十号 — August 30, 1990
二零一七年 二月十四号 — February 14, 2017

76

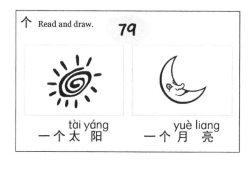

个　Read and draw.　**79**

一个太阳 (tài yáng)
一个月亮 (yuè liang)

有几个? Count by 个 and fill in the blanks.

hǎo péng you 三个好朋友　shū bāo 四个书包
qì qiú 六个气球　fēng zhēng 五个风筝

81

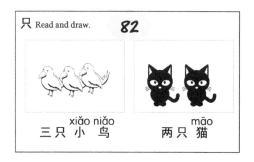

只　Read and draw.　**82**

三只小鸟 (xiǎo niǎo)
两只猫 (māo)

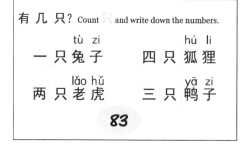

有几只? Count 只 and write down the numbers.

tù zi 一只兔子　hú li 四只狐狸
lǎo hǔ 两只老虎　yā zi 三只鸭子

83

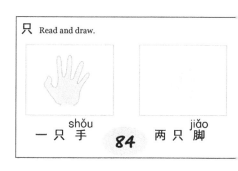

只　Read and draw.

一只手 (shǒu)　**84**　两只脚 (jiǎo)

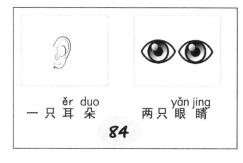

一只耳朵 (ěr duo)
两只眼睛 (yǎn jing)

84

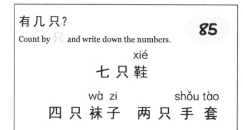

有几只?　**85**

Count by 只 and write down the numbers.

xié 七只鞋
wà zi 四只袜子　shǒu tào 两只手套

头　means head. Read and draw.

两头猪 (zhū)　一头大象 (dà xiàng)

86

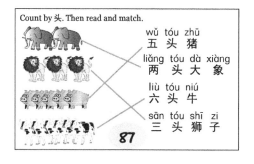

Count by 头. Then read and match.

wǔ tóu zhū 五头猪
liǎng tóu dà xiàng 两头大象
liù tóu niú 六头牛
sān tóu shī zi 三头狮子

87

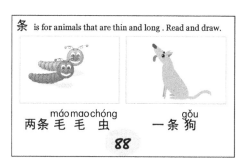

条　is for animals that are thin and long. Read and draw.

两条毛毛虫 (máo mao chóng)
一条狗 (gǒu)

88

有几条? Count by 条 and fill in the blanks.

yú 五条鱼　máo maochóng 两条毛毛虫
gǒu 四条狗　shé 三条蛇

89

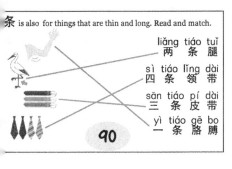

条 is also for things that are thin and long. Read and match.

liǎng tiáo tuǐ
两 条 腿

sì tiáo lǐng dài
四 条 领 带

sān tiáo pí dài
三 条 皮 带

yì tiáo gē bo
一 条 胳 膊

90

有 几 匹 Count by 匹 and write down the number.

mǎ
两 匹 马

91

Help the animals find their group.

tóu
头

pǐ
匹

zhī
只

tiáo
条

92-93

块 is for chunks or thick pieces. Read and draw. 94

qiǎo kè lì
一块 巧 克 力

xiàng pí
两块 橡 皮

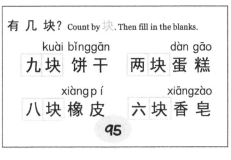

有 几 块? Count by 块. Then fill in the blanks.

kuài bǐnggān
九 块 饼 干

dàn gāo
两 块 蛋 糕

xiàng pí
八 块 橡 皮

xiāngzào
六 块 香 皂

95

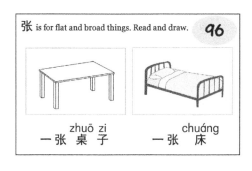

张 is for flat and broad things. Read and draw. 96

zhuō zi
一 张 桌 子

chuáng
一 张 床

张 is also for face and mouth. 97

liǎng zhī qīng wā   zhāng zuǐ
两 只 青 蛙， 两 张 嘴，

yǎn jīng   tiáo tuǐ
四 只 眼 睛， 八 条 腿。

sān zhī qīng wā   zuǐ
三 只 青 蛙，三 张 嘴，

yǎn jīng   tuǐ
六 只 眼 睛，十 二 条 腿。

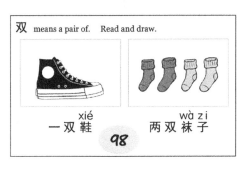

双 means a pair of. Read and draw.

xié
一 双 鞋

wà zi
两 双 袜 子

98

只 or 双? One, or one pair?

xié
三 只 鞋

ěr duo
一 双 耳 朵

chì bǎng
一 双 翅 膀

kuài zi
一 双 筷 子

99

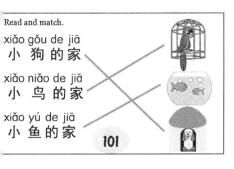

Read and match.

xiǎo gǒu de jiā
小 狗 的 家

xiǎo niǎo de jiā
小 鸟 的 家

xiǎo yú de jiā
小 鱼 的 家

101

Read and circle the correct answer.

102

shuí de yǔ sǎn
1. 谁 的 雨 伞 ?

dì di de   mèi mei de
弟弟的   (妹妹的)

shuí de fēng zhēng
2. 谁 的 风 筝 ?

jiě jie de   gē ge de
姐姐的   (哥哥的)

shuí de hú luó bo
3. 谁 的 胡 萝 卜 ?

xiǎo māo de   xiǎo tù zi de
小 猫 的   (小 兔 子 的)

shuí de zì xíng chē
4. 谁 的 自 行 车 ?

tā de   tā de
他的   (她的)

102

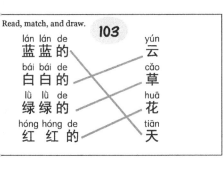

Read, match, and draw. 103

lán lán de   yún
蓝 蓝 的   云

bái bái de   cǎo
白 白 的   草

lù lù de   huā
绿 绿 的   花

hóng hóng de   tiān
红 红 的   天

Read, trace, and circle.

cháng cháng de bí zi
1. 长 长 的 鼻 子

yuán yuán de liǎn
2. 圆 圆 的 脸

jiān jiān de yá chǐ
3. 尖 尖 的 牙 齿

gāo gāo de gè zi
4. 高 高 的 个 子

104

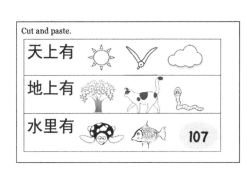

Cut and paste.

天 上 有

地 上 有

水 里 有

107

Fill in the blanks with the words in the boxes.

yǒu   gè   zhī   tiáo
有   个   只   条

shū bāo lǐ yǒu shén me
1. 书 包 里 有 什 么 ?

yǒu   māo
有 一 只 猫。

109

shù shàng yǒu shén me
2. 树 上 有 什 么 ?

píng guǒ
有 五 个 苹 果。

shuǐ lǐ yǒu shén me
3. 水 里 有 什 么 ?

yú
有 三 条 鱼。

109

Read the questions and circle the correct answer.

112

xiǎo māo zài nǎ lǐ
小 猫 在 哪 里 ?

zài shū bāo   hòu miàn   lǐ miàn
在 书 包   后 面   (里 面)

dì di zài nǎ lǐ
弟 弟 在 哪 里 ?

zài zhuō zi   xià miàn   páng biān
在 桌 子   (下 面)   旁 边

xiǎo niǎo zài nǎ lǐ
小 鸟 在 哪 里?
zài diànshì qiánmiàn shàngmiàn
在 电视 前面 上面
112

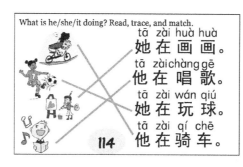

What is he/she/it doing? Read, trace, and match.

tā zài huà huà
她 在 画画。
tā zài chàng gē
他 在 唱 歌。
tā zài wán qiú
她 在 玩 球。
tā zài qí chē
他 在 骑车。
114

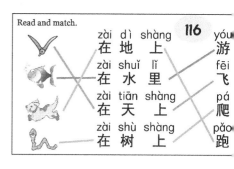

Read and match.

zài dì shàng
在 地 上
zài shuǐ lǐ
在 水 里
zài tiān shàng
在 天 上
zài shù shàng
在 树 上

116

yóu
游
fēi
飞
pá
爬
pǎo
跑

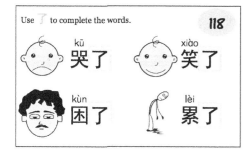

Use 了 to complete the words.
118

kū
哭了
xiào
笑了
kùn
困了
lèi
累了

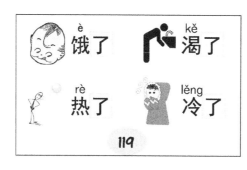

è
饿了
kě
渴了
rè
热了
lěng
冷了

119

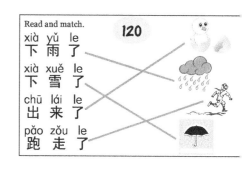

Read and match.
120

xià yǔ le
下 雨 了
xià xuě le
下 雪 了
chū lái le
出 来 了
pǎo zǒu le
跑 走 了

Read and draw.
121

gè zi gāo   gè zi bù gāo   yǔ dà   yǔ bú dà
个子高   个子不高   雨大   雨不大

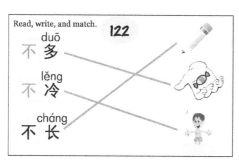

Read, write, and match.
122

duō
不 多
lěng
不 冷
cháng
不 长

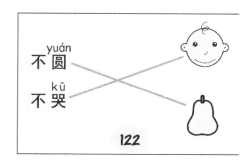

yuán
不 圆
kū
不 哭

122

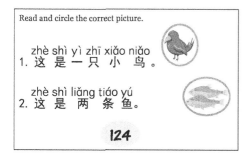

Read and circle the correct picture.

zhè shì yì zhī xiǎo niǎo
1. 这 是 一 只 小 鸟。
zhè shì liǎng tiáo yú
2. 这 是 两 条 鱼。

124

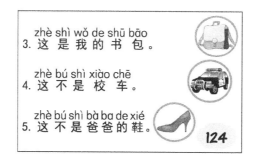

zhè shì wǒ de shū bāo
3. 这 是 我 的 书 包。
zhè bú shì xiào chē
4. 这 不 是 校 车。
zhè bú shì bà ba de xié
5. 这 不 是 爸爸 的 鞋。

124

Read and match.

huì xià dàn
会 下 蛋
huì wāng wāng jiào
会 汪 汪 叫
huì fā guāng
会 发 光
huì pá shù
会 爬 树

129

Read and match.

bǎ yǎn jing bì shàng
把 眼 睛 闭 上
bǎ hé zi dǎ kāi
把 盒 子 打 开
bǎ mào zi dài shàng
把 帽 子 戴 上
bǎ wà zi chuān shàng
把 袜 子 穿 上

131

Read and draw.

miàn bāo hé niú nǎi
面 包 和 牛 奶

132

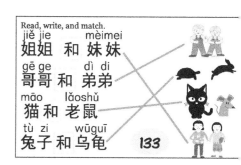

Read, write, and match.

jiě jie   mèimei
姐姐 和 妹妹
gē ge   dì di
哥哥 和 弟弟
māo   lǎoshǔ
猫 和 老鼠
tù zi   wūguī
兔子 和 乌龟

133

Congratulations!

祝贺＿＿＿＿小朋友！

你完成了《小手写中文》

学前班的学习。

特发此证，以资鼓励。

Are you ready for the next level?

Here are some characters that you've learned from this book. Read each character aloud and tell its meaning in English, or say it in a word/sentence in Chinese. As you go along, color in the boxes for the characters you know.

一	二	三	四	五	六	七	八	九
十	上	中	下	天	人	大	小	多
少	山	水	日	月	田	火	门	口
手	马	牛	羊	了	子	儿	长	衣
云	女	木	土	好	我	你	他	她
心	两	几	百	千	年	岁	个	有
只	头	条	张	块	号	飞	风	鸟
坏	的	在	不	是	吗	会	把	和

If you've colored 60 or more boxes, congratulations! You may now move on to the next level! If not, don't feel discouraged. Take some time to review this book. Once you are comfortable with the material, take this test again and sure enough, you'll move on!

Made in the USA
Columbia, SC
02 November 2020